Praise for G'Ra Asim's *BOYZ N THE VOID*

"Like any great mixtape, Asim's compilation is the most personalized of gifts. Layered, deeply revealing, it's a rhythmic journey through the indices, subgenres, and touchstones that encapsulate the refinement of an increasingly rare gem—black singularity. Written with love, erudition, and the utmost respect, *Boyz n the Void* is a genuine keepsake."

—Paul Beatty, author of *The Sellout*, winner of the Man Booker Prize and the National Book Critics Circle Award

"G'Ra Asim takes up a familiar form and brings it to new heights. His critical engagement with coming-of-age reflection adds refreshing depth, humor, and social commentary to a genre made immediately richer by his presence. *Boyz n the Void* is a spellbinding odyssey and a magnificent debut for an exciting young author and thinker."

—Kimberlé Williams Crenshaw, cofounder and executive director of the African American Policy Forum

"*Boyz n the Void* is the Black punk bildungsroman of your dreams: it's as if Bad Brains had written the smartest book in the world, only better. Asim guides us to the borders of American Blackness and beyond in this debut that's so mesmerizingly smart and so unsparingly honest it will literally rewrite the playlist in your heart."

—Junot Díaz, author of *The Brief and Wondrous Life of Oscar Wao*, winner of the Pulitzer Prize for Fiction

"G'Ra Asim's *Boyz n the Void* is full of dopamine hits and heartbreak. You don't want to stop listening, even when it aches. It becomes part of you. These essays are rigorous and tender and funny all at once, charged with humor that doesn't deflect from difficult honesty so much as it takes you deeper into the maze of truth. Asim is attentive to small acts of intimacy and solidarity and vulnerability—a punk kid parting the curtain of his mushroom haircut or learning to love the sweat and leather of a mosh pit—even as he dissects and illuminates, with searing, razor-sharp brushstrokes, the daily brutalities and hidden curriculums of structural racism. I'd gladly read anything by 'Ra the Exhorter—for his brilliance, his wit, his heart, and his electric illuminations of those forces of love and rebellion that might be able to remake our broken world."

—Leslie Jamison, *New York Times* best-selling
author of *The Empathy Exams*

"*Boyz n the Void* is a critical ethnography of growing up black and punk in the aughts. Asim strikes a balance between total immersion in the scene and the intimacy of a letter sent between brothers. *Boyz n the Void* manages to be ambitious, scholarly, and cool all at once—a testament to its necessity and authenticity. *Boyz n the Void* is essential reading for black weirdos, punks of all ages, and those invested in impeccably rendered American history."

—Cyrée Jarelle Johnson, author of *Slingshot*,
winner of the 2020 Lambda Literary Award in Gay Poetry

"In this wise, funny, and heartfelt meditation on the vagaries of post-conventional identity, G'Ra Asim writes that to be a successful black artist you 'must not only untether yourself from essentialized notions of blackness but create with such fluency as to move your audience to jettison the same constraints.' *Boyz n the Void* is many things—an impassioned paean to high-stakes cultural invention, a brutally honest excavation of the twenty-first-century color line, and a work of brotherly love—but it also marks the emergence of an important black artist."

—Chris Lehmann, editor of *The New Republic*

"There are just some voices that stop you cold, as resonances of some familiar brilliance but also of something so original, so compelling that you have no choice but to take notice. G'Ra Asim is one of those voices, and his book *Boyz n the Void: A Mixtape to My Brother* is the literary salve that we didn't know we all needed."

—Mark Anthony Neal, author of
Looking for Leroy: Illegible Black Masculinities

BOYZ N THE VOID

A mixtape to my brother

G'RA ASIM

BEACON PRESS
BOSTON

Beacon Press
Boston, Massachusetts
www.beacon.org

Beacon Press books
are published under the auspices of
the Unitarian Universalist Association of Congregations.

24 23 22 21   8 7 6 5 4 3 2 1

This book is printed on acid-free paper that meets the uncoated paper
ANSI/NISO specifications for permanence as revised in 1992.

Text design and composition by Kim Arney

Library of Congress Cataloging-in-Publication Data

Names: Asim, G'Ra, author.
Title: Boyz n the Void : a mixtape to my brother / G'Ra Asim.
Description: Boston : Beacon Press, 2021. | Includes
bibliographical references.
Identifiers: LCCN 2020035430 (print) | LCCN 2020035431 (ebook) |
ISBN 9780807059487 (hardcover) | ISBN 9780807059500 (ebook)
Subjects: LCSH: Asim, G'Ra, | African-American punk rock musicians. |
Punk rock musicians—United States. | African American authors. |
Authors, American. | Punk rock music—History and criticism.
Classification: LCC ML420.A919 A3 2021 (print) |
LCC ML420.A919 (ebook) |
DDC 782.42166092 [B]—dc23
LC record available at https://lccn.loc.gov/2020035430
LC ebook record available at https://lccn.loc.gov/2020035431

For the Asim team

To understand that you are black in a society where black is an extreme liability is one thing, but to understand that it is the society that is lacking and impossibly deformed, and not yourself, isolates you even more.

—AMIRI BARAKA

Tracklisting

Introduction

There's a sullen and brooding six foot two, 240-pound presence in my parents' house, and his shadow looms large over the otherwise placid nest. The presence is among the most timeless of American bogeymen—a black male in a state of rapid physical maturation. My folks regard the presence in a fashion that is heritage in their country of origin, which is to say, the presence is making them nervous. Having already reared three boys and one girl to satisfactory adulthood, my folks fancy their home as a factory of black excellence, and the lone remaining straggler on their well-trodden conveyor belt defies the troubleshooting best practices they've developed over thirty-four years on the job. My youngest brother, Gyasi, is a capable but disinterested student. Where other teenage boys chase girls and alcohol, Gyasi predominantly lurks indoors like some Wi-Fi–empowered Boo Radley. His communication with my parents is minimal, and when he does deign to acknowledge them, he alternates between withering sarcasm and charged silence. Gyasi teases my parents with glimpses of his intellectual and artistic potential but is recalcitrant when pushed to put his talents to use. Fourteen years apart in age, he and I are respectively the second- and fifth-born children of five and have always enjoyed a strong rapport, but even I have been of marginal help in allaying his malaise.

The familiar chorus of my mother's vexation is "I'm worried he'll be living in my house until he's forty." In fairness, it was not long ago that my mother fretted over a similar prognosis about me. I, too, was an academically withdrawn malcontent with an allergy to authority. My angst was both formless and easy to explain. I don't presume that Gyasi and I are exactly the same per se, but I can imagine he might be suffering from a crisis similar to the one that afflicted me as a teenager: an inability to envision a future in which a person such as he can fit comfortably into a ruthlessly competitive, anti-intellectual, anti-black society.

He could not be blamed for sensing the jarring discontinuity between the climate beyond his front door and the one in which he has been carefully incubated. Our father is an author and writing professor and our mother is a playwright, actor, and homemaker. Being raised by artists has not only shaped my and Gyasi's aesthetic leanings but also framed our perceptions of the American story. Our parents, both products of inner-city St. Louis, dropped out of Northwestern University in the late 1980s to return to the ghetto to raise my eldest brother and me. When not evading gunfire, Mom and Baba wrote and produced plays, organized poetry readings, and published literary magazines with their young sons playing at their feet. Our household was a fecund micro-bohemia situated incongruously within a warzone. As my parents' creative triumphs accumulated, our circumstances improved enough to move to the comparatively posh suburbs of Silver Spring, Maryland. Gyasi was born there. He's in some ways a beneficiary of a middle-class upbringing but is acutely aware of the Herculean feats it took for our family to produce such an environment and the precarity of sustaining it. After the economic downturn of the late aughts, our family relocated from Silver Spring to urban Baltimore. Gyasi briefly attended a public elementary school there until my parents grew so frustrated with the threadbare curriculum that they pulled him out in favor of homeschooling.

For the Asim children, living at the mercy of the economic peaks and valleys of my folks' artistic lives yielded a kaleidoscopic view of excess and indigence, oppression and opportunity. As a result, a grasp of heterogeneity is seared into all of our makeups. Gyasi and I, especially, are native dwellers of liminal space, and our experiences have often involved the exposure of unlikely confluences between distinct traditions, cultures, or ideologies.

My youngest brother and I lean on each other as intellectual sparring partners, creative collaborators, and confidants. We can't really afford not to. We're a generation apart but identify more with one another than anyone in either of our respective peer groups. The Asims are not unlike a twenty-first-century edition of J. D. Salinger's Glass family.

Like the clan that starred in *Nine Stories* and *Raise High the Roof Beam, Carpenters*, we're a close-knit but contentious family of bookish eccentrics struggling to reconcile our bohemian sensibilities with the prevailing norms of our era. My mother's unease about Gyasi's prospects for assimilation recalls Bessie Glass's concern for her youngest daughter in *Franny and Zooey*. When I reflected on Gyasi's coming of age, I thought of the Glasses' parallels and noted how the critical intervention of Franny's like-minded older brothers helps Franny to recover from an existential breakdown. In the book's conclusion, Zooey comforts Franny by explaining that even if no one around her appreciates her attempts to defy the insensitivity and superficiality of 1950s Connecticut, Jesus notices, and she must continue to lead a virtuous life to maintain the smile on His holy countenance.

Cue record scratch. That's not the kind of sentiment likely to galvanize my stringently empiricist baby brother. So what might our own version of the game-changing sibling-to-sibling pep talk look like? Even our parents seem to underestimate the vastness of the chasm between the value system of the house we grew up in and the broader culture in which we reside. Navigating that divide is no small task, but punk rock has been my unlikely lodestar.

I am not compiling a mixtape for the sake of indoctrinating my brother, of turning him into my mohawked spitting image. I'm making the mixtape because punk is fun, because a robust engagement with counterculture can serve as a vital antidote to soul-sucking normalcy, because remembering that you have predecessors who wrestled with many of the same riddles that you may wrestle with can help you feel that a roadmap to self-actualization exists. The result is part Nick Hornsby, part Ntozake Shange: my All-Time, Top-10 Angst-Neutralizing Punk Songs Because the Rainbow Clearly Isn't Enuf, Bruh.

Africa Has No History

An Annotation of Anti-Flag's "A Start"

Subject: The History of White People

Africa is not an historical continent; it shows neither change nor development, and whatever may have happened there belongs to the world of Asia and of Europe. . . . Nothing remotely human is to be found in the African character . . . their condition is capable of neither development nor education. As we see them today so they have always been.

—GEORG WILHELM HEGEL,
German philosopher, 1854[1]

At present there is no African history: there is only history of the Europeans in Africa, the rest is darkness . . . and darkness is not a subject of history. Please do not misunderstand me. I do not deny that men existed even in dark countries and dark centuries, nor that they had political life and culture, and purposive movement too. It is not a mere phantasmagoria of changing shapes and costumes, of battles and conquests, dynasties and usurpations, social forms and social disintegration. If all history is equal, as some now believe, there is no reason why we should study one section of it rather than another; for certainly we cannot study it all. Then indeed we may neglect our own history and amuse ourselves with the unrewarding gyrations of barbarous tribes in picturesque but irrelevant corners of the globe: tribes whose chief function in history, in my opinion, is to show to the present an image of the past from which, by history, it has escaped.

—HUGH TREVOR-ROPER,
British historian, 1961[2]

Africa has no history.

—JOHN KING,
sixth-grade history and English teacher, 2012

As Joan Didion famously observed, we tell ourselves stories in order to survive. The plausible corollary to this assertion is less often entertained: some especially durable fictions are designed to protect the prosperity, security, and psychic peace of some members of our civilization at the direct expense of others. Public high schools are a primary means by which such tall tales are transmitted. I got the above email from you on December 10, 2015. I was familiar with the last quote already, as you'd shared it with me a few years before. It was your instructor's curt reply when you had asked why your class had sections on Asian and European history, but nothing devoted to the continent your ancestors hailed from. Your inclination to constellate these quotes confirmed what I'd suspected all along—that some part of your underwhelming academic performance came down to a principled distrust of received wisdom. Where our mother, the Black Momba, might look at your middling freshman year report card and declare it "trifling," I'm tempted to call it discerning. "One factor that is always either overlooked or obscured in all interpretations of the low academic performance of Negro pupils," Albert Murray writes, "is the possibility of their resistance to the self-same white norms that they are being rated by."[3] Like Murray's intransigent rather than incapable Negro pupil, it was becoming increasingly clear to you that these slanted readings of history underwrote a distorted four-hundred-year-old reputation. I know what it is to experience public school as the crucible by which we forge a bleak status quo. Why open your mouth and say "ahhh" when the story at the end of the airplane spoon is tailored to ensure the survival of its authors while streamlining your own annihilation?

The ham-fisted excision of African history in your schooling doubles down on an identity vacuum that you are already fated to contend with. To haunt the halls of a high school as a black teenager is to be perceived as someone who is both dangerous and endangered. In the eyes of even your more generous stewards, your identity makes you a person uniquely vulnerable to threat and an embodiment of it.

A 2015 *New York Times* analysis of census data determined that for every one hundred unincarcerated black women aged twenty-five to fifty-four, there are only eighty-three black men between those same ages. The *Times* study casts those seventeen absent men, who for the most part are either incarcerated or casualties of violence, as "missing." This disparity is both raced and gendered, as the study found that only one white man was missing for every hundred white women. Of the 1.5 million black men missing from daily life, more than one out of every six are in jail.[4]

My suspicion is that adults who are even dimly aware of this sociological context see you as facing a problem so massive that you must, in some way, be complicit in it. If you are the same race and gender as these spectral figures, then surely you share other unseemly qualities with them that portend incarceration and untimely death. In his essay collection *The Disappointment Artist*, Jonathan Lethem addresses what he calls "the crisis of being so fraught with peremptory feelings in approaching a thing—a book, a movie, another person—that the thing itself is hardly encountered."[5] You don't need me to tell you that that crisis afflicts people like your sixth-grade history teacher. It may be only beginning to dawn on you, however, how often you will be the thing hardly encountered.

Black personhood remains a condition of unbecoming synecdoche. I say "personhood" rather than "manhood" because although gender shapes how we experience this substitution of the part for the whole, no black person is exempt. A black person is less often received as a singular being of unique dignity and value than a shadowy composite of vices and deficiencies.

I emphasize "unbecoming" because we aren't all getting a bounce in the polls from Barack Obama's or LeBron James's exploits, but we incur demerits per the alleged misdeeds of black people we'll never meet. The symbolism of that AWOL 1.5 million men overshadows you without being a physical presence. Those missing brothers lost to violence or incarceration take up more psychic capital in the social imaginary than people like you and me, people who have not disappeared, people in the flesh before their very eyes and actively pursuing full, vibrant lives.

For these reasons, your email was a non sequitur and yet right on time. You were fourteen years old. *Aw, look at my baby brother shrewdly identifying Hegel, Trevor-Roper, and his sixth-grade teacher as links in a chain that binds him and me and others like us to the mirage of black pathology,* I'd thought sardonically. *They grow up so fast!*

That kind of critical engagement with received wisdom is not only legible to me as resistance. It is the essential ingredient in the mortar with which I've built a self.

The power of the stories others tell about us to survive is not unlimited. If dramatic irony occurs when the audience knows what the reader doesn't know, then "post-conventional identity" occurs when a character knows what a story's omniscient narrator does not. Post-conventional identity is what I see as a kind of practical triangulation between Charles Cooley's looking-glass self, Lawrence Kohlberg's post-conventional morality, and W. E. B. Du Bois's double consciousness.

Cooley tells us we develop self-perceptions based on how others see us. How we are treated becomes the measure of who we are. Via his own coinage of double consciousness, Du Bois points out that this method of identity formation is

treacherous for subordinate groups because our social interactions are more like fun house mirrors. To be black is to be
privy to largely unreliable indicia of who you are.

I've come to think of identity the way Kohlberg writes
about morality. He conceived of morality as something that
exists in three stages: pre-conventional, conventional, and
post-conventional. Children nine years old and younger occupy the pre-conventional stage, during which morality is
shaped largely by the punishments and rewards doled out
by adults. Most teenagers and adults, on the other hand, are
in the conventional stage, where they absorb normative values without much reflection or examination. That's the phase
I would liken to Cooley's looking-glass self—passive acceptance of society's judgments. Kohlberg's third stage of morality is the one with the fewest adherents. Most people never
reach it. Those who do attain the post-conventional stage
choose their own principles and think through moral views
for themselves.

To be to the point, Gyasi, I began to transpose Kohlberg's third stage to the question of identity as a matter of
schoolyard necessity. A lifetime of being called "oreo" and
"white boy" by people of all races demanded a consolidation
of my blackness at a tender age. To view one's racial identity as beholden to a specific set of aesthetic tastes seemed a
tacit concession to some of racism's most pernicious fictions.
If racism is a force that organizes not just economic and political realities but social ones, it follows that the prevailing

understanding of black identity might not be the one that best serves the pursuit of a fulfilling life.

It is, of course, adaptive to internalize what the mass cultural looking glass tells you about blackness. Survival necessitates some awareness of the four-hundred-year-old reputation that precedes you. But post-conventional identity provides a kind of metaphysical sustenance no less important: a vision of the self that is not self-evident.

When I think about the genesis of my personal investment in post-conventional identity, I think about an inside joke I had with myself in high school. By senior year, I still had yet to earn a driver's license and the void in my Dickies wallet irked me. So I filled the space where a license might go with a self-styled form of identification. I carried around a three-by-five index card on which I had scrawled with a black Sharpie,

Card-carrying member of the radical punk rock intelligentsia

The kernel of this joke was convoluted, but I figure it tickled my teenage funny bone for some combination of the following reasons:

1. As the unrepentant owner of a 2.2 cumulative GPA, I had no objective basis to count myself among any "intelligentsia."

I've never actually seen anyone give a teacher an apple. So it seemed like something I should eventually do."

Ms. Thompson stared at the apple in silence for a few moments before accepting it. I could almost hear the tinkling piano music that must have been playing in her head.

"Oh, I know," she said in a pinched voice. "It's fun to play with signifiers and tropes like that, isn't it?" She sniffed. Her watery blue eyes grew wetter than usual. They threatened to leak outright.

"Thank you so much, G'Ra. This really means so much to me." She hugged herself and bowed slightly. "More than you know."

It wasn't long after the apple gift when I realized my mistake. I had misled Ms. Thompson, charmed her into assuming that I was a student whom she could expect to meet the basic expectations of a competent pupil: completing the assigned reading, attending class regularly, contributing to discussions. In reality, my adolescent unease was in full bloom, and I quickly established myself as the worst performing student in AP Literature. The sense of urgency that animated my high-achieving classmates escaped me. College admissions season loomed, but get-it-together speeches from our parents, from guidance counselors, and eventually Ms. Thompson herself were less persuasive than the Anti-Flag lyrics blaring from my headphones. My approach to public education answered the call sounded in "A Start," the first track on your mixtape.

Look, singer/guitarist Justin Sane might not have anticipated that any egghead black teenagers would take the brisk, minor-key, critical-thinking fight song on 2001's *Underground Network* literally, but this was shortsighted.

> *Your prison warden is your school*
> *Training you to be a social screw*
> *Stage a jailbreak, swim against the flow*
> *Show those motherfuckers what you know!*

Tension arose between Ms. Thompson and me as she slowly began to recognize my unfitness for the role of teacher's pet. Her confusion was understandable, her disappointment justified. When I managed to attend class, I could be spotted perusing a thick anthology of British Romantic poetry in the moments before the bell rang. My notebooks, while consistently bereft of completed homework assignments, harbored copious pages of my own extracurricular writing, much of which was composed as Ms. Thompson lectured unheeded a few feet away. When Ms. Thompson assigned Edwidge Danticat's *The Farming of Bones*, I mentioned offhandedly that I'd met the author ten years before, when Baba had organized a reading series, in our hometown of St. Louis, in which Danticat had participated. The anecdote delighted Ms. Thompson—that is, until she noted the abysmal scores I registered on reading quizzes about the book.

Our ostensible kinship deepened Ms. Thompson's sense of betrayal at my disengagement from her class. The two of us even happened to rock matching electric orange dye jobs. Mine, a bathroom sink concoction of drugstore dye, took the from class was apparently an excellent way to do justice to Ralph Ellison's counterhegemonic intentions.

"You're not here to learn, you just want to contradict me," Ms. Thompson accused. "This is a place of learning and you're not taking that seriously."

Sure, it's definitely a place of some kind of learning, I thought, shoveling my belongings into my bookbag and pushing my chair into my desk. *But what kind? And to what end?*

The clash between Ms. Thompson and me was so ripe with allegorical overtones that it strikes me as surreal when I now recall it. I don't describe the confrontation as any kind of post hoc justification for my teenage insolence. I'm not trying to glamorize my academic floundering. I was a bored, frustrated, depressed seventeen-year-old who needed a shrink and a hug (maybe you know something about how that feels, eh brother?), and my antics were tantrums as much as they were informed dissent. But I did recognize public schools as repositories of received "wisdom," as machinery designed to facilitate the maintenance of a social and political status quo that marginalized and persecuted people like me. And I was deeply ensconced in an oppositional subculture that I interpreted as an ethos for exactly this kind of transgression. Punk's snarling skepticism activated, empowered, and validated me. The songs and the spirit were a live studio audience's clamorous applause as I walked out of AP Literature class that day, deafening whoops and catcalls that nonetheless failed to puncture the bubble of unreality in which I'd acted out. I should've been thinking about how Mom and Baba, who at that time were thoroughly humorless when it came to academics, might react to the news that I'd been thrown out of class for the umpteenth time. But mainly I was thinking of the chorus to "A Start."

Reciting back their facts and numbers
—That don't make you smart.
There's much more to intelligence
And thinking for yourself would be a start!

Weeks later, Ms. Thompson sat me down to defend her choice to give me an F for the semester. It was a preemptive defense, as I had not disputed the grade and didn't plan on it. She did not offer the usual admonishment about working harder and being more organized. Her disappointment appeared to stem primarily from the perception that I was acting out of character.

"You're not the kind of person who has any business *failing* AP English," Ms. Thompson lamented. "You're supposed to be an artsy punk kid." She ran her hand through her bright orange tresses before nodding at my own.

"With goofy hair," Ms. Thompson added.

For once, I kept my mouth shut. I didn't clarify the causal relationship between being punk and failing English.

Challenging Ms. Thompson about Ellison felt like getting some crucial licks in on an invincible video game boss. It was not my first brush with omniscient narration, and by seventeen, I suspected that moral victories were the best one could hope for. When I got your email, Ms. Thompson sprung to mind as a parallel incarnation of the well-meaning, well-educated master narrator. The tea is that she probably fancied herself a cannier, more ethical breed than the men you called out. For all her liberal, antiestablishment posturing, Ms. Thompson was an uncritical enforcer of a majoritarian view of the world. Keats's influence had gone only so far with her; his notion of Negative Capability had not compelled her to incorporate any "uncertainties, Mysteries, doubts"[6] into her unqualified distillation of black American writing. Her awareness of Ellison and Danticat only caused her sanctimony to balloon. She was unwilling to concede the possibility that Ellison's take on African American life is but one interpretation. Her schooling had equipped her to dismiss my lived experience out of hand. The narrative of African American literary culture was, to her, what Maurice Blanchot said applies only to the nonliterary book: "a stoutly woven web of determined significations."[7]

It's not hard to account for where Ms. Thompson might be coming from. Depending upon where one wants to set the bar for this kind of thing, one might even credit her for merely being familiar enough with a seminal black book to overstate its significance. It was 2005. That uber-popular Chimamanda Adichie Ted Talk about the dangers of a single story hadn't yet become the main jam of progressive culture warriors everywhere.[8] I may be ungracious to paint Ms. Thompson as some kind of unwitting villain. Beneath the proper lighting, her actions might be construed as gallant. I think it mostly depends on who is telling the story.

Your own pursuit of self-knowledge seems particularly fraught at this cultural moment, when white nationalism and black normcore are having a simultaneous epoch. Both phenomena are indebted to the truncated history at which your email pokes fun.

When a cavalcade of revanchists descended upon the University of Virginia campus around midnight on August 12, 2017, they chanted, "We will not be replaced." While the looming destruction of a statue of Robert E. Lee was the immediate catalyst for the neo-Nazi hootenanny, the choice of rallying cry reflected a broader crisis. The rise of black normcore likely contributes to the perception among white men that they are an increasingly marginal class being phased out and supplanted by traditionally disadvantaged groups.

New York Times critic Wesley Morris described the mundanity of the spectacle: "Hundreds of men—*young men*—(and some women) marching in the night. Watching the way photography froze many of their faces into a rictus of rage was chilling. Some of that dismay came from seeing how perfectly basic they were—or what, about nine months ago, you might have called 'normcore.' Almost everyone who walked by any camera looked like a classmate or an acquaintance."[9]

Their fears are outsized, but not beyond comprehension. In some form of twisted kismet, Jay-Z's long form music video for the track "Moonlight" dropped just days before the calamity in Charlottesville. The short film actualizes the brownification of a hallowed white cultural touchstone. Hov takes the familiar archetypes from *Friends*, one of the most successful TV franchises of all time, and recasts them using black actors. The rapper turned mogul's vision of the show does not demand a broadening of its narrative universe. It merely accepts the existing premise of the show and replaces alabaster figures with melanized ones. Comedian Hannibal Burress makes a brief appearance to skewer the limitations of such a formula. Asked by Jerrod Carmichael, who plays Nubian Ross, to give his honest assessment of the proceedings, Burress calls the project "garbage. Terrible, man. Wack as shit."[10] Carmichael stammers a defense, mumbling that "when they asked me to do it, I was like, all right, this is something subversive, something that would turn over on its head." It's a telling admission: race weighs so heavy as a signifier that taking a mass cultural phenomenon and altering that single variable can be forgivably confused for a credible subversion. Even the most benign expressions of blackness, including those calibrated to be the mirror images of whiteness, are received as inherently deviant. Burress's criticism has some affinity with Elizabeth Chin's in her essay "Ethnically Correct Dolls: Toying with the Race Industry. " After completing an ethnographic study of ten-year-old black girls in working-class New Haven, CT, Chin suggests that the children's resourcefulness in the absence of black Barbie dolls is best understood as a practice of "race-queering." Chin observes that Mattel's 1991 introduction of ethnically correct

Barbies—figures of varying skin tone, anatomical build, and facial features purportedly based on African American faces—may have been intended to redress issues of representation, but ultimately had the effect of solidifying racial boundaries in the public imagination. In fact, Chin argues, the children's race-irreverent modes of play with white Barbie dolls actually provide a better schematic for the disruption of prescriptive racial boundaries than the advent of "ethnically correct" dolls themselves. The first two and a half minutes of Jay's "Moonlight" video are the sitcom equivalent of Mattel's introduction of ethnically correct Barbies in the early '90s. *Friends*, like Barbie, is a beloved household name brand among white and black America alike, and using black actors to portray its story could be the same clumsy stab at inclusion. It would not represent "the bending, twisting and flipping of apparently real or natural or accepted social states" that Chin credits the working-class black girls in New Haven, Connecticut, with achieving.[11] If the imaginative reconstruction of race and blurring of consensus categories is race queering, the black *Friends* schtick is an example of its off-brand cousin, black normcore.

Jay-Z's clip for "Moonlight" is in on the black normcore joke, but black normcore is not always so self-aware. Popular television shows like *Insecure*, *Blackish*, and the Rachel Lindsay season of *The Bachelorette* epitomize the black normcore formula without the wink. It's worth cataloging its propensities: black normcore can be both, in Burress's words, (a) "wack as shit" and (b) a literal realization of a bunch of white nationalist lunatics' darkest fears. This might be because normalcy is contested territory. There is less consensus about what is normal than is commonly assumed. A shared disdain for normalcy is one locus of the unnerving synchronicity between punk culture and the latest iteration of virulent conservatism. "Alternative" status has great rhetorical utility; every point of view is more seductive when pitched as having a niche appeal that escapes the benighted plebes who are invested in its opposite. Punk rockers and the alt-right both fancy themselves as footloose fringe dwellers resisting a somnambulating middle. (People who call themselves "woke" are operating from a similar premise.)

Where punkness is pliable enough to be a rebellion against anything you can name, the alt-right's choice of prefix is intended to distinguish itself from conservative movements of yore. Both of the two subcultures refer to their antagonists as "normies." Normcore might be an exonym in the same way "politically correct" is. One often defines normalcy in order to cast one's self in opposition to it. Of course, if you're black, it's a lot harder to imagine that being racist, sexist, and xenophobic makes one a dissident. To the vast majority of even mildly attentive black people, the alt-right is a white-supremacist cover band, the trite rehashing of an immortal scourge as banal as the Beatles. While many white people get indignant about the alt-right as if hoary supremacists represent some kind of aberration from the shape of American history, black people receive their breathlessness the same way many white people might if you'd only just heard and were floored by *Sgt.*

Pepper's Lonely Hearts Club Band in the 2010s. It's not that *Sgt. Pepper's* is unworthy of awe and tongue clucking; it's that treating it as a novel discovery, rather than as something foundational to a canon, is obtuse and ahistorical.

The alt-right's characterization of those outside their ranks as "normal" is not complete nonsense, however. It's true that a formulation in which active investment in white supremacy and normalcy are divisible from one another is enough to make Hannah Arendt face-palm from the grave. But there's legitimacy to the idea that taking up tiki torches against a sea of imagined troubles represents an alternative to the soft complicity of the masses. "Normies," in the alt-right sense, are people happy to benefit from a stacked deck so long as they do so beneath a veneer of civility. Punks and the alt-right ultimately agree that both groups are dissenters from a tepid center. The critical difference is that the politics of that center more closely resembles that of the alt-right. Black normcore, like ethnically correct Barbie dolls, offers a black incarnation of the base-camp America that both punks and the alt-right look down their noses at.

Though I'm sure he'd be appalled at this addition to his legacy, it's almost like black normcore takes its cues from Saul Bellow. Toward the end of his life, Bellow's critiques of multiculturalism anticipated the rhetoric of the alt-right—and dovetailed with your teacher's preening dismissiveness. He once asked an interviewer, "Who is the Tolstoy of the Zulus? The Proust of the Papuans?" as if ethnic groups are all competing in some kind of eternal culture Olympics and Aryans are waxing everyone handily.[12] It's not merely the assumption that one group is dominating the medal count that is problematic but the very terms of the contest. In an essay about the poetic construction she calls "subsumptive analogies," Katy Waldman chastises Bellow not for his racial hubris but for his choice of phrasing. "If garden-variety similes serve to equate two things, these lopsided comparisons force one term to exert twice the gravitational pull of the other," writes Waldman.[13] She's right, but Bellow's choice of construction is no incidental slip of the tongue. His wording reflects the Western understanding of race. As your schooling has already begun to illustrate, Gyasi, black people's experience is *generally* narrativized in terms of subsumptive analogy. Consider, for instance, the framing of American racial progress, which is usually condensed into something like, "We've come a long way, but still have a long way to go."

Yet black folks are no more human today than they were at the time of the Three-Fifths Compromise. There were black people capable of sitting at the helm of the empire centuries before 2008, when white people finally condescended to elect one president. We regularly conflate white people's grudging, belated recognition of black humanity with black people's achievement of social equality. Contending with the gravity deficit Waldman describes is a fundamental predicament of black experience. This is perhaps the crux of what makes black normcore what it is: culture that willfully reinforces the normative subsumption of blackness into a foil for whiteness.

Fiscally speaking, it's nice work if you can get it. Issa Rae, creator and star of HBO's *Insecure*, is developing a brand off the "X of the Y" construction. I watch her ascent with some ambivalence, aware that the worlds she builds probably don't accommodate someone like you, even as she advertises them as your home turf. "I would like to pitch you a new show about black teenagers," Rae says in a video for the *New Yorker*. "Think *90210* or *Gossip Girl* for black kids. . . . I don't think since, like, I would say *Moesha*, have we followed the lives of black teens."[14]

Rather than challenge the tribalist underpinnings of a question like Bellow's, black normcore hustles to conjure up a Zulu Tolstoy. Black normcore begins from assumptions outlined by Hegel and Trevor-Roper: there's a *them*, there's an *us*, and there are cultural materials that belong exclusively to each. (There's at least a whiff of this stench on Ms. Thompson's prescriptions about Ellison.) I certainly understand the inclination to furnish evidence of one's own equality, and that's probably why black normcore often feels like the fumbling retort to a bully's jeering. If answering Bellow's smug challenge is black normcore's operating principle, then Ralph Wiley's all-world clapback at Bellow is in keeping with the race queering ethos. "Tolstoy is the Tolstoy of the Zulus," he writes, "unless you find a profit in fencing off universal properties of mankind into exclusive tribal ownership."[15] Wiley's solution to the Bellow conundrum chimes with Elizabeth Chin's advocacy for race queering. Chin's essay on ethnically correct dolls is essentially praising children who rightly intuit that Mattel is the Mattel of New Haven.

Black people's relationship to normalcy is admittedly hard to parse. It's one of the many unwieldy elements of the idea that sociopolitical position and identity are totally coextensive. Clearly black people come in many varieties, including "extra regular." Some elements of mass culture nonetheless invoke blackness as a symbol of totalizing otherness. For some of those who are not black, alienation is not a component of blackness but the condition by which it is singularly defined. Morrissey, punk/emo icon and noted blabber of racist inanities, once sold a merch design featuring James Baldwin's face encircled by the Moz lyrics "I wear black on the outside because black is how I feel on the inside."[16] The multivalence of the word "black" makes it difficult to pin down which chromatic associations Morrissey claims to identify with. Does he feel like someone who is lonely, mysterious, and dramatic on the inside? Or does he feel like someone who is habitually followed around department stores? The decision to impose those lyrics over Baldwin's mug suggests that Moz believes there is an affinity between loneliness, mystery, and drama and black identity. The shirt invites a murky commingling of both the racial and nonracial connotations of blackness. One wonders if they are ever actually extricable in the popular imagination.

The former Smiths frontman gets at least one thing right. Black clothing enjoys a unique status in rock 'n' roll counterculture. More than once I have glanced around the crowd at a show and felt that the throng of black T-shirt wearers was masquerading in a state of visual nonconformity for which I had been involuntarily and permanently tapped by merely existing. Perhaps that impression is the other side of Morrissey's same self-dramatizing coin. Morrissey thinks he identifies with James Baldwin based on the fact that Morrissey is weird and alienated from other white people. This almost sort of makes sense, but lots of people are weird and alienated *in addition* to being black and don't see their blackness as the beginning and end of that alienation. One may be black and no more disenchanted with pop culture than with the most visible and revered aspects of black culture. Just because you don't watch *Friends* doesn't mean you stand for *Living Single*. By the same token, legions of black folks are painfully straitlaced. But somehow, I'm thinking black clothes on a white person aren't really a means of telegraphing identification with someone like, say, Herman Cain, the black Tea Party activist and anti-masker who succumbed to the coronavirus after attending a Trump rally.

o o o o

Such is our lot as heirs to a continent expunged of legacy. We're camped out in passages that unreliable narrators redact for their survival. I urgently want you to know that the living here can be good even if it's never easy. I like to think Anti-Flag is here to help. At its best, punk is a mnemonic for retaining what you know and what the narrators refuse to know. They need not be replaced, but, better yet, you need not be subsumed.

Evidence of Things Unscene

An Annotation of Propagandhi's
"Less Talk, More Rock"

Somewhere in an alternate universe in which hip-hop's general listenership is literate enough to remember a bit character from *Invisible Man* and I am a socially conscious firebrand of an emcee rather than a steezpunk singer-songwriter, my rap name is 'Ra the Exhorter. Here in the sector of the universe I actually inhabit, my alter ego 'Ra the Exhorter is a mere escapist fantasy. The cultural conditions that would make such a persona legible to more than four or five people do not exist, but I daydream about them nonetheless. Of course there are thoughtful, literate, politically astute rappers, and naturally there are hip-hop aficionados who are receptive to that sensibility. But achieving broad currency as the Exhorter could be a tall order in view of the prevailing trends of commercial hip-hop—and the robustly anti-intellectual mass culture of which hip-hop is an influential part. I can't help but equate choosing to operate in 'Ra the Exhorter's mode with laboring to learn a language that lacks a critical mass of native speakers. It's not that I would actually prefer to be an emcee instead of a rock musician. I would just enjoy living in an America that could easily contextualize 'Ra the Exhorter's aesthetic.

During grad school I took a class on narrative long-form journalism. In it, the professor touted the importance of "aestheticizing your personality." Even more than compelling language or intensity of perception, the professor argued, how well a writer managed to sublimate her personality into a text was crucial to the quality of the writing. I found the assertion persuasive but wondered if aestheticizing your personality is made more or less difficult based on circumstances beyond the writer's control. Exhibit A was the rascally headshot on the back of Ander Monson's collection of essays, *Neck Deep and Other Predicaments.* Looking very much like a literary Zach Galifianakis, the author is pictured unkempt and unsmiling, his hair and beard protruding erratically in a style his barber might call "panhandler chic." Monson's prose is rather consistent with the impression one might generate from the jacket photograph. His writing is indulgent, self-obsessed, unapologetically shallow, and littered with libidinous digressions. It's also quite good. Though Monson is a skilled enough prose stylist that it would be reductive to attribute the success of his work to any single element, the aestheticization of his personality is key to his approach. I don't think it takes anything away from him to acknowledge that he is blessed with a personality that is easy to recognize. Schlubby, navel-gazing, impious white men preoccupied with unattainable women are American cultural mainstays. Enlivening the words on a page by channeling George Costanza is nice work if you can get it—in no small part because Costanza's familiarity does about half the work for you. For those of us who do not cohere with time-honored archetypes, cultivating a dynamic prose persona requires more heavy lifting. We are to a greater extent at the mercy of the reader's imagination. Our audiences have not been inundated from birth with primers for our proclivities. Studying creative nonfiction in a master's program seemed at times like a contest to devise the most dynamic prose selfie. I have been hamstrung by the fact that in order to conjure a literary photograph of myself, I must first prove that I exist.

My experiences in nonfiction workshops have illustrated the point with deflating clarity. During the same semester, I enrolled in a workshop led by a popular nonfiction writer. The writer is known for provocative, first-person essays about her soothingly unremarkable life as a lower-middle-class Midwestern white woman who moved to the big city in pursuit of literary stardom. Like Monson, she is an undeniable talent, but her style finds broad traction in part because she represents a familiar and innocuous perspective. The problems and ideas in her work flatter a particular view of the world. My time as her pupil suggested that the conventionality of her prose persona informed her sensibilities as a reader.

After reading each of my first two workshop submissions, the professor announced to the class that she'd determined I was "sending myself up" in both of my pieces. Before my classmates began their critique, the professor said she wanted to establish a particular interpretive foundation. It was important that we discuss my submissions in view of something the professor had deduced: the narrator in my work must have been a satirical voice the writer (me) had adopted to mock himself. Without qualification, she told the class that the writer's voice was "improbably sensitive, thoughtful, and self-aware" and thus I must have embellished those qualities for some obscure rhetorical purpose. I, the human behind the pen, apparently seemed an implausible figure. Thus, I could only be understood as an exaggeration, a caricature, a chuckle-worthy device. During both of these workshops, I was leery of coming across as a neurotic, defensive artist and so I protested only mildly at first. Eventually I grew more emphatic as the same bizarre responses to the essays piled up. Unsurprisingly, my insistence that the voice was earnest and not meant to be satirical was to no avail. It was a swift illustration of how easily an invisible man can become an inaudible and illegible one.

Subsequent workshops of my essays followed a similar pattern, and the professor's conviction that my actual personality was an elaborate pretension persisted for the entire semester. Like clockwork, after each of my submissions, the instructor and celebrated essayist urged me to unlock my "authentic voice." My narration, she insisted, would read more honestly if only I "wrote how [I] talk." I couldn't be sure, but it was tempting to conclude that I was actually being asked to present a characterization of myself and a narrative that validated the preconceived notions she had about people who look like me.

That same spring, you were in eighth grade and working for your middle school newspaper. The articles you pitched and turned in reflected your vast range of interests as I knew them—the arts, business, tech, public health. But your newspaper advisor was skeptical that your contributions to the paper were original work. Having proofread some of your articles and helped you brainstorm others, it was easy for me to imagine the source of her confusion. She likely couldn't make the clarity of thought and precision of language on the page jibe with the observable characteristics of the person standing in front of her. It probably didn't help that you are an Artist-in-Reticence—by which I mean, a person who doesn't always outwardly perform his intellect for public consumption. Each time you turned in a new piece, the advisor insisted that you tell her who had actually written it for you. You maintained that the work was yours. The advisor's suspicion never waned. Eventually, you told the Black Momba that you intended to quit the newspaper at the earliest opportunity and wouldn't bother with journalism again. Your argument wasn't lost on me. What's the point of presenting yourself and your thinking authentically on the page if incoherence with black stereotypes makes your writing inadmissible to the white gaze? My impulse was to tell you to buck up, to stick with journalism despite the adversity. Any pursuit you chose would present similar obstacles, race-related and otherwise. But I was chagrined to realize that I was experiencing a parallel nightmare in my writing workshop. The void, it seems, is not something one ages out of by default.

Your appearance was viewed as so incongruous with your work product that the most plausible explanation for the "discrepancy" was that you plagiarized. The solution to the "riddle" that my own appearance and creative work presented was that the latter was necessarily satirical. My horrified recognition of that unhappy convergence—between a teenage black artist facing roadblocks to finding his voice and a young adult encountering a scrambled version of the same impediments—was the catalyst for your mixtape. Punk and straight edge culture have served for me as the kind of "esthetic equipment for living"[1] that Albert Murray argues African Americans en masse have found in blues music. The continuities between your experience and mine—across the supposed generation gap—suggest that punk might function as equipment for navigating exactly the kinds of conundrums you're likely to face as you come of age as well.

It is a peculiar form of invisibility to have one's deliberate self-definition and disclosure flatly dismissed for its noncompliance with racist expectations. Vivid, honest, and thoughtfully rendered as a black self-portrait might be, it is competing for real estate in imaginations, white and otherwise, which are largely monopolized by the phantom projections of ethnocentrism. And yet I don't quite blame my audience, your newspaper advisor, or my professor. You and I have no representatives on TV. We are not in the news. There are no stock characters in movies to which you and I are tidily compared.

Using the sensibility of an invisible person to invigorate prose in an inviting, accessible way is like trying to break into Top 40 radio by playing free jazz. Like it or not, one necessarily contends with two interdependent, concurrent responsibilities: to entertain the audience and to expand its limited palate. The critic Margo Jefferson calls it imagining what hasn't imagined you. To be a black artist of any consequence, you must not only untether yourself from essentialized notions of blackness but create with such fluency as to move your audience to jettison the same constraints.

It follows that my exploits in punk rock are beset by similar challenges. There's rarely been any such option as blending in with the punk scene—a crowd of black sheep doesn't camouflage a black body. The reflection of myself that I heard in punk music, that I recognized in lyric sheets and liner notes, that I felt in the solidarity of a circle pit, all contradict the foreignness connoted by my skin. The security of my claim to punk as something that belongs to me, something to which I am indigenous, has always been tenuous. So I've searched for ways to plant a flag and declare my sovereignty over some marginal corner of the punk landscape. Calling the music that I create "steezpunk" is one such effort.

Steez is an amalgamation of style and ease, a slang word especially prominent in '90s hip-hop. The term encapsulates a form of effortless cool, a *never-let-them-see-you-sweat* credo that positions exerting strain and embodying hip as inimical to one another. Marrying black slang with "punk," a word fastened securely with connotations of pasty whiteness, is my way of representing the confluence of black experience and punk experience. "Steezpunk" is the word for when your black and punk experience have always been coextensive. It's a rallying cry for when the seemingly unlikely intersection of the two is at the crux of who you are. My conception of the term was somewhat indebted to Charles Bukowski's observation that "style is the answer to everything."[2] If the riddle is how to be black while engaging with a cultural tradition ill-equipped to accommodate blackness, steezpunk is the solution. In coining "steezpunk," I hoped to devise an ethos for the unshakeable awareness that your way of speaking, walking, existing confounds a certain normalized a priori shape and a roadmap for the business of perpetrating this defiance with panache and self-possession. It's a catchphrase translated from the parlance of bone knowledge. A taxonomic rank to locate myself within a pantheon not expecting my inclusion.

Creating under the mantle of steezpunk is also a choice that is informed by my extensive observation of punk and its various permutations. In indie music culture, artists often conjure hype by dreaming up corny portmanteaus to mastername highly specific, dubiously extant subgenres. You may be the only person on the globe consciously making "scumfolk," for instance, but founding a subgenre can become a self-fulfilling prophecy. A sticky enough name will find its way to musical acts it can cling to. Homespun buzzwords like "chillwave" and "easycore" have become entrenched landmarks in counterculture, thumb tabs for perusing the unknowable legions of garage band wannabes. I submitted "steezpunk" to Urban Dictionary with the aim of legitimizing a term that codifies my experience as a self-aware black person who has been a punk rocker for more than half his life. I wanted to see the word validated, immortalized, engraved in cyberspace in order to ground myself. I wanted an online compendium of slang and euphemism to concede that I exist. Having freighted my submission with so much psychological weight, I was, of course, destined for disappointment.

Thanks for your definition of steezpunk!

Editors reviewed your entry and have decided to not publish it.

To get a better idea of what editors publish and reject, sign up as an Urban Dictionary Editor here: http://www.urbandictionary.com/game.php

URBAN DICTIONARY
steezpunk

A smarter, jauntier spin on punk pop. Boisterous and irreverent but with an emphasis on wit. Combines crunchy guitars and adhesive pop melodies with the literate lyricism, punchlines and wordplay of 90's "backpack" rap.

> "I don't listen to a lot of rock bands, but the ones I do are mostly steezpunk."

I don't doubt that there were credible reasons not to include "steezpunk" in Urban Dictionary. Still, it was impossible not to take the rejection personally. *You are not recognizable,* the rejection letter seemed to say. *Your suggested neologism is a word without a referent because you aren't real.*

The Pulitzer Prize–winning Dominican American author Junot Diaz has lamented the consequences of living without cultural materials that represent your experience. It is no accident that Diaz's work depicts individuals who might otherwise elude mass cultural radar.

"If you want to make a human being into a monster, deny them, at the cultural level, any reflection of themselves," Diaz said in an address to students at New Jersey's Bergen Community College in 2009. "And, growing up, I felt like a monster in some ways. I didn't see myself reflected at all. I was like 'Yo, is something wrong with me? That the whole society seems to think that people like me don't exist?' And part of what inspired me, was this deep desire that before I died, I would make a couple of mirrors. That I would make some mirrors so that kids like me might see themselves reflected back and might not feel so monstrous for it."[3]

When Urban Dictionary opted not to ratify steezpunk, I resolved to make a zine about my band, *babygotbacktalk*. I enlisted your help. We held an impromptu editorial meeting at the dining room table about the zine's direction. You were responsible for hand-cutting the images and text to fit the eight-paneled frame. I didn't inherit the steady hands and keen eyes of our visual artist paternal grandfather like you did. Before I finalized the content and sent it to the family printer, you looked it over and made suggestions. The zine included a definition of steezpunk and its relation to *babygotbacktalk*'s mission statement. In a way, reifying my—and to some degree, your—experience in analog form was more gratifying than giving steezpunk a Google presence. A zine is tangible, material culture. Zines can be portable, easy to disseminate, and inexpensive to produce. We didn't talk about how hand-folding the *babygotbacktalk* zines and passing them out to strangers felt like a physical realization of the operative metaphor in the phrase "cultural production." For me, it was manufacturing and spreading culture in the most satisfyingly Marxist sense. There was something appealing about feeling ink on my fingers that was spilled in the service of an aesthetic goal: to fashion an externalized self slim enough to fit in my back pocket like a hand mirror.

o o o o

Assessing the terrain of the known universe, physicists Enrico Fermi and Michael H. Hart were boggled by a needling question. If there were nonhuman, sentient beings somewhere out there in space, why hadn't they revealed themselves to us?

As Fermi and Hart saw it, all signs pointed to the conclusion that human beings are not alone in the universe, yet there was no observable proof of the existence of extraterrestrial life. The resultant quandary became known as the Fermi paradox.

The evidence was this:

- The Sun is a typical star, which means there are myriad other stars in the galaxy that are far older.
- Probability would suggest that some of these stars would be orbited by Earth-like planets. If Earth is as typical as the Sun, intelligent life could evolve on some of these planets.
- Developed Earth-like civilizations could likely achieve faster-than-light travel, a technology that humans targeted as early as the twentieth century.
- Interstellar travel at even a relatively slow pace would allow for the colonization of the galaxy in a few tens of millions of years.[4]

"Where is everybody?" Fermi wondered aloud, looking out into the lonely cosmos in 1950.

○ ○ ○ ○

In one section of the *babygotbacktalk* zine, I define steezpunk by listing things that it isn't. The initial draft included "comment sections" as an example of things that are not steezpunk, and you circled it in red marker.

"This is too corny," you explained dryly.

It didn't make the final cut. You were right. Any denizen of twenty-first-century cyberspace is well aware of the unmitigated horror of comment sections. Only the most masochistic among us wade into the cesspool of non sequitur responses, inscrutable ravings, and ad hominem attacks. It is a sort of armchair sociological impulse, however, that inspires my forays into the infamously grumpy peanut gallery at Punknews .org, a site to which I contributed interviews throughout most of my twenties. The Org is something of an iconic punk site. Its influence among the Warped Tour set is such that the site has spawned its own variant of punk music: "orgcore," which is characterized by gruff, weather-beaten vocals, sneakily adhesive melodies, and lyrics by turns maudlin and introspective. Bands who hang their hats on that formula, such as Dillinger Four, Hot Water Music, Strike Anywhere, Alkaline Trio, and others, are all but unilaterally adored by the Punknews.org readership. According to the rock culture satire site yourscenesucks.com, an archetypal orgcore punker rocks a neckbeard, ill-advised tattoos of the Alkaline Trio insignia, flannel shirts, cutoff shorts, and black caps strategically placed to conceal thinning pates.

If the orgcore community can be boiled down to a code of homogeneous sartorial choices, it at times seems to be equally conformist in its ideological leanings. A particular exchange in the Org's comment section about *23 Live Sex Acts*, a live album from orgcore forerunners Against Me!, typifies the strain of tepidly liberal, cisgender groupthink that is as endemic to punk as liberty spikes.

Goes one Org commenter:

Solid track but Laura talks way more than in the past. The thing that I loved about Against Me! was that they got straight down to business, took you by the throat and didn't let go until the last encore. [The talking on this live track] wasn't egregious, but ya know . . . come on.

Chimes in another:

i was an against me [*sic*] apologist well through [their 2010 album] white crosses and thought that her coming out as transgender was very compelling and i thought it would be interesting how it would shake things up, and legitimately glad that she made a decision relative to her happiness and well-being, but i wasn't prepared for the post 2011 against me "transgender manifesto" that was to follow, now one of my favorite bands has been utterly coopted [sic] by identity politics.

Writes a third commenter:

I completely understand what you're saying, but I still dig the band. The songwriting is as good as it's ever been, even if the lyrics aron't completely relatable. I imagine that the transition will not be at the front of her mind for the rest of her career and the songs will go back to being more political in nature.

It has been three years since Against Me! vocalist and scene heavyweight Laura Jane Grace, formerly Tom Gable, announced her transition. In an exclusive 2012 *Rolling Stone* cover story, Grace revealed that she'd struggled with gender dysphoria for most of her life and had finally resolved to begin living as a woman. Her coming out was a high-profile litmus test for punk: how would a cis male-dominated community that prided itself on its progressive nonconformity respond to the front person of one of its iconic bands becoming a woman? At the time Laura Jane Grace came out, Caitlyn Jenner had not yet graced the cover of *Vanity Fair*. Actress and LGBT advocate Laverne Cox had yet to make her debut as transwoman prisoner Sophia Burset on *Orange Is the New Black*. The term "transgender" had only begun to penetrate the national lexicon. Eighteen months later, the Gainesville, Florida, quartet would release *Transgender Dysphoria Blues*, their sixth studio album and a watershed moment in punk rock history.

The aforementioned commentary on *23 Live Sex Acts*, Against Me!'s first full-length release since *Blues*, speaks to the results of that litmus test. The good news: brazen, overtly bigoted responses were relatively rare. (Which isn't too much of a surprise, right? When it comes to aughts-era prejudice, sneak dissing is what's hot in the streets.) The bad: Grace and company's strident trans advocacy has consistently been met with a familiar and undue condescension. For all its radical bravado, punk remains prone to replicating the social hierarchy of the dominant culture it purports to undermine. White cisgender males are the patrician class of punk, the default vantage point from which punk lyrics are expected to speak.

To single out *Transgender Dysphoria Blues* as an exercise in identity politics is to overlook the angsty white dude slant of the vast majority of seminal punk records in history. Against

Me! are offenders not because the lyrics report from a particular social location but because *Transgender Dysphoria Blues*, down to its very title, unapologetically centers otherness. One wonders if anyone ever accused NOFX, the SoCal punk luminaries behind whiny, first-world-problems anthem "Don't Call Me White," of engaging in identity politics simply by virtue of writing songs that reflect an awareness of their social positions. It's hard to imagine anyone dismissing Minor Threat's "Guilty of Being White" for referencing the racial identities of the band members that composed it. Hell, Grace's own band didn't raise any eyebrows with "White People for Peace," a protest song released five years before her coming out that pointlessly centralizes dissenting Caucasians as if they are the foremost demographic opposed to war. A band is only speaking out of turn or confounding punk orthodoxy when it addresses a concern beyond the scope of white cisgender maleness.

The suggestion that Against Me! will return to themes "more political in nature" on future albums is revealingly nonsensical. In the eyes of the Org loiterers quoted above, a record that challenges a transphobic establishment and disrupts the primacy of cissexual narratives is not "political." The implicit assumption seems to be that Against Me!, a band known for its anarchist politics and scathing social commentary prior to Grace's transition, has diverted from its ideological wheelhouse by writing a record about gender dysphoria. Hoarse-throated tirades against government, war profiteering, and corporate greed—hallmarks of the Against

Me! discography—are acceptably political topics. Addressing a minority experience constitutes an indulgent digression.

These types of attitudes shortchange punk's potential as a revolutionary mode. Punk, as a community and tradition that views itself as an alternative to the prevailing value system, can provide a framework for enlightenment through purposeful decentering. The simple beauty of a DIY punk show is its rejection of a top-down model. Band and fan unite on equal footing. The line between each is willfully blurred. In theory, at least, a culture of inclusion and camaraderie creates the opportunity for punks to broaden their worldviews via exchange with people they'd be unlikely to engage with in a stratified mainstream. Realizing this possibility requires a willingness to countenance what is not immediately "relatable." It demands the patience to interpret art that does not serve as a mirror, a temperament that was the price of the ticket for my particular involvement with punk (and perhaps Laura Jane Grace's) in the first place. The wariness of some Org community members toward *Transgender Dysphoria Blues* illustrates a key source of my occasional frustration with punk's limitations. Listeners are too often seeking in punk rock an echo chamber of their own dominant group perspectives, dressed up in a hollow guise of dissent.

I was in attendance for Against Me!'s triumphant 2014 appearance at the Higher Ground Ballroom in South Burlington, Vermont, two weeks before the ambitious quasi-concept record's street date. The show was part of the northeast leg of the band's first tour since their frontwoman's transition.

Grace commanded the stage with a newfangled exuberance, her six-foot-four frame looming larger with the addition of bombastic high-heeled boots. The Ballroom crackled with the electricity of radical change happening in real time as the band ripped through a mix of old favorites and songs from the new album that dealt explicitly with Grace's journey toward self-actualization. I lunged into the pulsating mass of euphoric, deodorant-averse whiteness that thrashed jubilantly in front of the stage. I wrapped my arms around bearded, beer-bellied punk lifers that screamed along. Near the end of the set I made eye contact and exchanged knowing grins with the band's singer-guitarist during the customary encore jam of "I Still Love You, Julie." That song's refrain, "Maybe somehow this scam / can still save us all," echoed with new significance as Laura Jane Grace and I beamed back and forth, a pair of sore thumb punks upping each other.

○ ○ ○ ○

Punk and Afrofuturism are linked to me, if for no other reason than learning about them felt like finding the diagnosis for a condition I'd clearly come down with long before I knew there was a name for it. Both are vessels for the clever inversion of received wisdom, for the critical examination of dreary, unquestioned norms. Afrofuturism is a literary and cultural aesthetic of radical reimagining. It typically combines elements of science fiction, magical realism, and fantasy to revise and remix established notions of Afrodiasporic experience. (Though I didn't know it at the time, my coinage of steezpunk has some kinship to Afrofuturist rhetoric. And 'Ra the Ex-horter is definitely an Afrofuturist emcee.) Dominant figures in the tradition include the painter Jean-Michel Basquiat, novelists Octavia Butler and Samuel Delaney, and legendary funk ensemble Parliament-Funkadelic. Afrofuturist literature and art often draw parallels between prototypical alien abduction stories and the kidnapping of Africans during the slave trade.

Prior to discovering Afrofuturism as an ongoing discourse with an identifiable tradition, our sister, Indigo, and I had long been fond of comparing ourselves to extraterrestrials as a metaphor for totalizing otherness. Where some immigrants to the United States are somewhat derisively characterized as FOBs (Fresh Off the Boat), Indigo and I have each at one point or another described ourselves as "fresh off the mothership." We have immigrated from a planet on which critical thinking doesn't scare the average person shitless. Where basic compassion is a reasonable expectation. Where energy, irreverence, and imagination are not anathema to the dominant culture. As the actual descendants of persons kidnapped from their homes on a foreign continent and forced to labor under draconian conditions for the benefit of their captors, we are subject to clear, lasting social and historical forces that contribute to our alienation. We are links in a genealogy that makes science fiction tropes convenient symbols. But Fresh Off the Mothership is a shorthand for a soul-deep disfranchisement that being heir to historical atrocity only begins to explain. Being Fresh Off the Mothership is a condition that encompasses differences other than race but is at once circumscribed by it. It is a form of self-mythology intended to address the nagging feeling that your default setting for negotiating the world creates an unnavigable chasm between you and those around you. It's a summation of the feeling that you're shut out of a social reality by virtue of a fatal allergy to the Kool-Aid that's widely, insatiably guzzled to maintain the grand delusion.

In the Fresh Off the Mothership formulation, our embrace of our former home's value system compounds the challenge of assimilating with the alien civilization into which we were unceremoniously dropped. Of course, the practical explanations for my and our sister's perennial outsiderhood are myriad and boring. They may include: an upbringing in a household of dramatically fluctuating income yet permanently overflowing with books; a sense of gender identity unbound by traditional binaries; liminal positions in a family hierarchy with three other siblings, a live-in grandma, a non-interventionist Art Dad and a domineering, stay-at-home Art Mom; the comfortable embrace of tastes and interests contrary to racial stereotypes but counterweighted with nonchalantly pro-black political stances. Using Fresh Off the Mothership as a code to articulate these characteristics provides the vital opportunity to acknowledge being anomalous without de-centering one's self. Different mustn't always mean marginal. If we've just been accidentally abandoned by the mothership, there exists a context in which our strangeness is venerable, admirable, endearing, even if that context is twinkling distantly somewhere in infinity on high.

The persistent sensation of being "other" within all social groups, regardless of the specific demography of the setting, makes for a tangled relationship with punkness. Can you expect to achieve belonging among punks, by and large a group of people who curate and embellish an affected dash of difference, when your own marginalization is an ontology?

Being a black punk rocker is about maintaining a feat of punk rock inception. You are a punk among punks, a subversion of rules that themselves are subversions of yet other rules. At the same time, black people and aestheticized irreverence are a more intuitive fit than is popularly acknowledged. I would be hard pressed to think of anything more definitional to blackness than being subject to the chafing of oppressive norms. That punk is an ethos for telling such norms to go fuck themselves always seemed, to me, a miracle. Who would more naturally gravitate to a subculture that idealized otherness than a people whose otherness was inscribed permanently upon their bodies? Or so was my naive logic as an adolescent punk. The makeup of the scene never reflected this purported synchronicity between punkness and blackness. Whatever the soundness of the basis to expect otherwise, the numbers simply never bore it out. Looking out into the crowd from a stage I shared with four white bandmates or scanning the snow blindness-inducing pages of *Alternative Press*, I was compelled to wonder aloud:

Where is everybody?

Until I made contact with Mars, I wondered whether I was alone in the universe.

○ ○ ○ ○

I happened upon Propagandhi's *Less Talk, More Rock* at a moment in my life that lent itself to being totally fucking bulldozed by the record. The Winnipeg-based punk legends are a trio on their 1996 sophomore album, recorded prior to the addition of second guitarist David Guillas. The muscular, hooky skate punk instrumentals make an apt vehicle for frontman Chris Hannah's fiery polemics.

Even the album's title was a decree that was apropos for me that summer. I could not have been more tired of talking. I'd recently told our parents about the sexual abuse I'd suffered at the hands of a relative as a child and had concealed for twenty years. It was the first time I'd acknowledged the aftershocks of that experience—trouble forming attachments, asexual leanings, seemingly random bouts of anger, and self-loathing—to anyone other than our eldest brother, Joe. A fissure had widened between me and one of my oldest friends because he'd grown tired of my passionately anti-oppressionist attitude. He was sick of my being what he called "a social justice warrior," an accusation he leveled with the venom one might reserve for a slur. (The latter incident made Propagandhi's album opener "Apparently I'm A 'P.C. Fascist'" hit particularly hard. I was both comforted and unnerved that a PC fascist might have been the mid-1990s version of a social justice warrior, but finding out that Hannah had been derided for the same thing meant I was in good company.)

At twenty-eight, I was highly aware of the commonplace assumption that melodic punk was something I should have outgrown, an inherently juvenile form devoid of substance and only of fleeting relevance for teenagers. The folly and popularity of this assumption made the act of blasting the record from iPad speakers in my late twenties all the more deliciously defiant. The album's lyrical themes are anything but trite and disposable. Fast, catchy screeds about the frustration of living in a culture too distracted, lazy, and complacent to confront its own pathologies were my theme music to the Charleston shootings, to the suspicious July 2015 death of Black Lives Matter activist Sandra Bland, to the unceremonious execution of Sam DuBose during a routine traffic stop in Ohio. The contrast between *Less Talk, More Rock*'s enduring poignancy and the perceived vestigiality of the tradition from which it hails underscores Propagandhi's criticism of Western society: ours is a civilization too deluded to even appreciate the cultural production that encourages precisely the kind of consciousness-raising we so desperately need.

I was particularly taken with the title track and its cheeky celebration of the band's triumph over normative masculinity. As a trauma survivor just beginning to confront the gnarly details of my victimization as a child, I found myself with a lump in my throat as Hannah sneered the track's archly empowering punchline:

All the fists in the world can't save you now
Because if you dance to this, you drink to me
And my sexuality
With your hands down my pants by transitive property

The seminal Fat Wreck Chords release sports cover art that boldly announces the record and its creators as "Animal-Friendly, Anti-Fascist, Gay-Positive, Pro-Feminist," modifiers I am genuinely moved to see in print. But there is something unsettling about the glaring absence of an adjective declaring the band's regard for black lives, or an affirmation of their vested interest in dismantling the systems that uphold and perpetuate white supremacy. At the risk of indulging some anthropomorphist bigotry of my own, the omission of any mention of anti-racist sentiment feels yet more egregious when the band's sympathy for nonhuman beings is first in the litany. Yes, the record was released in 1996, nearly two decades before the phrase "black lives matter" became vernacular. Yes, the band's lyrics challenge ethnocentrism and name structural inequality as endemic to capitalist American life. But the exclusion of the descriptor "Anti-Racist" feels conspicuous. Maybe it's a petty ax to grind, but in an era in which the seemingly innocuous declaration that "black lives matter" is a source of endless controversy, it's hard not to read into the fact that even a band as irreverent as Propagandhi was skittish about centering black life in the struggle for justice.

o o o o

"Mmm, it smells like punk in here!" I announce, walking into the YMCA in Cambridge, Massachusetts, for the annual Smash It Dead Fest. And boy, does it. The telltale stench of body odor, cigarettes, and leather, which permeates the sticky summer air, conjures so many mosh pit memories, so many sweaty, electric nights in basements and clubs. The uninitiated would recoil at the scent of this intemperate upstairs YMCA recreation room turned Punk Rock HQ; it is the olfactory corollary of the acquired taste. Its presence sanctifies the space for me, however, and I am immediately confident the scene is set for an excellent performance by Aye Nako, the headliner I'm there to see live for the first time.

I couldn't discover Aye Nako, a band that refers to themselves as "four weirdos trying to find their confidence/ sexuality/harmony/payday," until I was well into my twenties. The members and I are similar in age, and I like to think we led parallel punk lives before they formed their band, that we all grew up in the scene feeling a love and a lacking in equal parts. The Brooklyn four-piece bills their music as "sad punk songs about being queer, trans and black." Even reading that simple elevator pitch on the band's Facebook page is galvanizing for me. I am heartened at seeing punk's freak flag gripped tightly with hands that belong to someone whose sociopolitical reality is veritably freakish. I'm glad I stayed punk long enough to encounter Aye Nako, to watch their popularity grow, to feel satisfied at their warm reception in the scene.

In a 2015 interview with fanzine *The Miscreant*, Aye Nako singer-guitarist Mars Ganito confirms the profound extent to which he and his bandmates are singing my life with their words:

> A good chunk of last year was hard for me as a black person. I broke down many times as I learned the growing list of names of black people beaten, mistreated, and murdered by police and vigilantes across the country.... I wrote a song called "White Noise" about how whiteness is centered in everything, how it taught me to hate myself for being black, how when I was a kid I used to pray to God that I could be white, how my Filipino mother didn't think it was necessary or important to teach me to speak Tagalog [so] that way we can come off as American, aka white as possible, how it scares me that white supremacy doesn't even need white people to perpetuate it, and how white people are going to demonize me for saying any of this out loud because how dare I ask for respect, for more than the bare minimum.
>
> I wrote a song about my experience with being a victim of child sexual abuse. For the first several months, it sucked to sing this one because I was thinking about my trauma every time I sang it. Every single time we ran through it, I thought about how fucking alone I was as a kid and not a single adult came to my rescue.[5]

Experiencing Aye Nako at Smash It Dead Fest in the summer of 2015 is like a resolution to the Fermi paradox at last. *Here* is everybody. That's not to say the gig is jam-packed with black folks, only that the setting has ceded some ground to make a place in the middle for otherness, that willful decentering is, for once, the name of the game.

Eccentrically coiffed people of dubious hygiene sporting denim vests populate the YMCA. Septum piercings and quirky eyeglasses accentuate an array of asymmetrical faces. Doc Marten boots and Converse sneakers adorn ankles contorted in gawky, lurching dance moves. Their owners nod, sway, and flail spastically to songs from Aye Nako's brooding, moody EP, *The Blackest Eye*, a collection more indebted to noodly '90s indie rock than the more straightforward pop punk of the band's earlier offerings. Perusing the wares at their merch table, a new T-shirt design catches my eye. The shirts feature the band's name written in a stark, understated script and flanked by a pair of broad-nosed, full-lipped humanoid figures with four eyes each and otherworldly scaled skin.

"If you like aliens and black people, we've got some cool new merch," Mars quips in between songs, laughing. A tall, visibly energized black girl near center stage whoops an affirmation, while the rest of the majority-white audience shifts uncomfortably or offers feeble half smiles. As one of three black people in the crowd, I am tempted to offer a similar "we out here" gesture, but the irresolution of the moment pleases me, so I just grin silently. The room's ambient discomfort foments a temporary telepathy.

Should we make sure he knows that we do like black people? you can almost feel the showgoers wondering.

○ ○ ○ ○

I couldn't know for sure whether Mars connects aliens and black people for the same reasons I would. I can't tell you that everyone in the audience understands that they are witnessing anything out of the ordinary for punk rock, that banging your head in any way demands engaging your brain. I don't even know that Aye Nako's new T-shirt design is intended to represent the experience of crash landing on unfamiliar terrain, aghast at your displacement but slowly, carefully, constructing a place for yourself within it anyway. I do know that for a few moments, on this night, in this place, I am back on the mothership.

Marching Through the Mosh Pit

An Annotation of Operation Ivy's
"Room Without a Window"

It was the week of Freddie Gray's death, and an announcement circulating on social media let me know that New Yorkers were organizing in solidarity with Baltimore. Unsure of whom, if anyone, might be a Black Lives Matter sympathizer among my graduate school cohort and not eager to scarlet-letter myself as a militant Negro, I'd traveled to the march alone to meet up with Rachel, a radical friend from college who had been my marching buddy at a previous protest. When I got off the train, a middle-aged white woman in jeans and a T-shirt eyed me thoughtfully, having guessed my destination.

"Hey," she said, stepping directly into my path. "Are you headed to the march or are you just walking through the park?"

"I'm attending the march," I replied.

"Good, because African Americans are the people who really need to be out here," she said, narrowing her eyes. "I've been seeing mostly white people and it's really *you all* who need to turn out more."

You got the sense she believed she'd softened her pushy admonishment simply by opting for "African Americans" rather than "blacks." (Or, I suppose, another more verboten word she really wanted to say.) I assured the patronizing stranger that black citizens would, in fact, be present in numbers as they consistently had been throughout my participation in Black Lives Matter events. Thinking she'd perhaps been prey to the deception of the "eye test" at some prior demonstration, I added over my shoulder that "we're only thirteen percent of the population as it is."

I followed the sound of makeshift activist drums to an area on the other side of the park, where a swelling crowd was coalescing in the square. A palpable energy permeated the space as New Yorkers of all stripes laughed and joked, vented and commiserated. Rachel and I coordinated over text messages, and she sidled up beside me in the crowd once we'd agreed to meet in front of a giant poster memorializing people of color killed by police. Oversized hoops dangled from her ears, long enough to ricochet off the dimples she made prominent with the smile she flashed me in greeting.

"Yo, thanks so much for meeting me down here, R. Hill," I said, giving her a sideways hug. A veteran of the Occupy movement, Rachel was an old pro when it came to demonstrations.

"No problem, of course. I'm excited to hang with you!" Rachel enthused. "I figure we'll march for a couple hours, smash the state, then finish off the night with some Chipotle!"

You had to love the woman's zeal.

The march hadn't started. Many people had clearly come straight from their jobs, putting aside fatigue, hunger, and general vexation with their day to delay their returns home in favor of mobilizing for justice. Rachel played with her phone while I paced around restlessly, observing the demographics of the demonstrators with the gauche white lady's comments echoing in my mind. But it didn't take long before I found one of my people.

I extended my hand to the wiry, twentysomething in high-top Vans sneakers and skin-tight black jeans. An electric pink and yellow Exploding Hearts T-shirt hugged his torso. The cover art to the ill-fated Portland punk quartet's sole studio album, *Guitar Romantic*, was emblazoned across the front. In addition to their penchant for indelible pop melodies, the Exploding Hearts are known for their tragically prophetic band name: three of the four members, all in their early twenties at the time, were killed in a car crash in 2003, mere months after the release of their lone studio album. In death, the departed members of the Hearts have transmuted into eternal symbols of dashed potential, of the fragility and preciousness of youth in emergent bloom, glittering inkblots on to which we are free to project as we please. "Hey bro, I like your shirt," I said to my counterpart. "I was just listening to that record on the way down here. It fucking rips."

"Thanks, man," he said, and in the brief moment that our hands clasped we formed a hokey avatar of transracial reconciliation, his pasty fingers curled snugly around my nougat brown palm.

"I like your shirt too, dude." He gestured at the logo for the band Bomb the Music Industry! that adorned my own chest. I was sporting a tee featuring a photo montage of Bomb the Music Industry! on tour, with the years 2004 and 2013 separated by a hyphen, as if on an epitaph. The grainy screen printing was in keeping with the band's fiercely DIY ethic, but the blurry photos hardly did justice to the raucous, sweaty, sublime experience of seeing the Baldwin, New York, collective live.

"They ruled, man. Sucks they broke up," my fellow punk lamented. "My name is Jake."

"I'm G'Ra," I told him, and he took on that look of bland incomprehension that comes over people when I introduce myself. No matter. My name wasn't really all that important—we had already recognized each other as a kind of kin that transcends names, colors, languages.

"I'm always happy to see other punks out here, showing solidarity and resisting apathy. It means a lot."

Jake nodded.

"Totally, bro. It's good to see you here, too."

I lost Jake in the sea of bodies that began to queue up in alignment with the predetermined route for the march, but our brief encounter set the tone for that night. Throughout the demonstration for Freddie Gray I'd spot other Black

Lives Matter protesters in Dead Kennedys or Black Flag or the Flatliners T-shirts and stop to acknowledge them. The fist bumps we exchanged were singularly galvanizing, a wordless affirmation of the overlap between punk rock attitude and progressive citizenship. To see punks taking a stand against state-sanctioned murder, against the structural inequity in Baltimore that had manifested in days of urban calamity that dominated national news, was to witness proof that our subculture's ethos of informed dissent was more than mere posturing.

Of course, punk has core values in common with most iterations of black struggle in Western history. But in the movement for black lives that emerged around the time of Trayvon Martin's death in 2012, the choices of tactics and rhetoric have seemed to me to be, well, way more punk. The fundamental aims of black activism a century ago and those of today are, unfortunately, more similar than not. W. E. B. Du Bois published *The Souls of Black Folk* in 1903. Insisting that we have souls is essentially litigating the same claim as declaring that our lives matter. Where today's generation departs from its predecessors primarily has to do with the burden of proof. As Bree Newsome observes in her essay "The Civil-Rights Movement's Generation Gap," "a feature of the modern movement has been an open rejection of 'respectability politics'—the notion that black Americans must prove themselves 'respectable' to gain equal rights."[1] As a punk, I applaud the abandonment of any strategy that assumes we might secure the recognition of our humanity via rigid adherence to white norms. It strikes me as a validation of the same thought process that allowed me to comfortably ignore black norms.

"Whoa, that's like my goal," Rachel breathed. "To be able to walk up to someone and say, 'It's good to see other punks at protests' and have them recognize me as like them." She laughed breezily in a way that was part mockery, part genuine amazement. Not for the first time, my mind wandered back to the long, circuitous path that led me to this point: existing, and for the most part, reveling in the middle cell of a three-ringed Venn diagram most people wouldn't think existed.

"So what's up, man—you think you don't gotta pull your weight helping us set up just because you got a broken leg?"

Kevin Powell stared at me expectantly. The former *Real World* breakout star spoke with the affectation of someone who owned his reputation as a hip-hop generation figure-head. Being a good friend of our dad's, he was showing off his *ability to relate to young people* by teasing me with deadpan humor. I often got the sense that I confused or possibly irritated adults by defying their attempts to get me to crack a smile. I'm reminded of this phase of my life every time I watch you interact with adults, Gyasi. I'm unsurprised that you seem to have the same tendency. It's not that I tried to be obstinate per se; it was more that generating a comparably sardonic retort came more easily than showing my teeth.

"It's not the broken leg," I shot back, gesturing at the thick, forest-green cast that began at my left ankle and ended a few inches above the knee. "I just have a latent helping instinct. It should kick in slightly after all the work is done."

Kevin, Baba, and a handful of other writers were assembled at Vertigo Books, an independent bookstore in Prince George's County, Maryland. The owner had arranged a reading and signing to promote the 2000 release of *Step into a World*, an anthology of poetry and essays edited and compiled by Kevin Powell and featuring a contribution from Baba. While the writers and Bridget arranged chairs and folding tables in preparation for the event, I wandered off to the front of the store to peruse the goods. At thirteen, I was accustomed to bumping shoulders with the literati. I'd grown up on the small yet vibrant literature, visual, and performing arts scene in St. Louis, Missouri, where our parents were either hosting, organizing, or performing in arts-related functions more weekends than not. Being an observer of and participant in a bohemian subculture had already shaped me in a lasting way. The Black Momba, an actor, director, and playwright, is fond of saying that I attended my first poetry reading at six months old. I was a dude for whom an opportunity to browse through the considerable selection at Vertigo was better than being DiCaprio at a Victoria's Secret model sleepover.

Schlepping along on my crutches, I scanned the nonfiction titles until one paperback caught my eye: *The Philosophy of Punk*. I was intuitively attracted to both "punk" and "philosophy" as buzzwords, but seeing them in combination was too much to resist. Based on a casual perusal of Minor Threat and Crass MP3s a classmate had pillaged on Napster, I was already vaguely aware of the discordant, uninviting sounds of punk rock, and I understood it to be an acquired taste. I had a sense that some nebulous set of antiestablishment ideas was key to the whole thing, but the possibility that punk could be understood as a philosophy was instantly appealing to me. Resting my weight on the two metal appendages propped under my armpits, I balanced the book on the tip of the Vertigo bookshelf and dove into *The Philosophy of Punk.* Just as I'd suspected, punk wasn't all sound and fury signifying nothing. As author Craig O'Hara framed it, punk was a rich countercultural tradition founded and perpetuated by enterprising, disaffected young people. It was an idea more than a sound; a nonconformist ethos that championed progressive individualism over rote adherence to received wisdom.

Uncovering the essence of the movement via the cold, impersonal engagement of a text set a precedent that would remain consistent throughout my experience as a punk rocker. The social component of punk culture played a minimal role in my attraction to it, and would continue to have only cursory influence in my participation in punk as I matured. The few kids at my middle school who sported spiky hair and wallet chains seemed to relish their belonging to an insular and opaque counterculture, one associated with a sound that seemed more like the aural equivalent of spitting on the listener than wrapping them in a welcoming embrace. Punk rockers who were already initiated weren't going to be agents of my conversion. There was no solicitation from like-minded peers, no clique of neighborhood kids urgently recruiting me to join the mohawked rank and file.

What was more, African American presence in punk rock was, as far as I knew, virtually unheard of. I had never personally encountered so much as a single nonwhite punk. The only indication that anyone of my melanin quotient could dig on power chords and double-time drums was Mos Def's namedrop of legendary all-black punk bands Bad Brains and Fishbone on his 1999 track "Rock 'n' Roll," a meditation on the history of the white plundering of rock music from its black progenitors. (Prior to happening upon O'Hara's book, I'd noted Mos Def's reference with interest to Joe, who at the time was a hip-hop aficionado utterly mystified by my curiosity about punk. "You're wondering about a reference," our eldest brother sniffed, "that he made on the wackest fucking song on the album.")

But punk's gruff, exclusive, unapologetically monochrome exterior hadn't deterred me. If anything, it egged me on. I was itching to learn the secret handshake requisite for admission to what appeared to be the most glamorously transgressive anti-club around. It didn't bother me that no one had beckoned me forward with a crooked finger and whispered the password in my ear; I knew that hopping the fence and sneaking in through the back door was more in keeping with punk's aesthetic anyway. There was a paradoxical yet pleasing logic to the idea that I was a trespasser in a subculture that was itself stridently irreverent of prevailing attitudes about belonging. As a precocious and often bullied adolescent, I'd already come to terms with the fact that immersion in the world of ideas was a low-risk, high-reward alternative to the perils of social relationships. By thirteen I was quite accustomed to more easily finding reflections of myself in texts than in conversations. Maybe a lifetime of crowd-surfing, circle-pitting, and early onset tinnitus wasn't what LeVar Burton had in mind in the *Reading Rainbow* theme song, but "take a look / it's in a book / I can be anything" was a message I took to the bank. It was only fitting that I would stumble upon the countercultural tradition that would profoundly shape my life the same way that I'd learned about virtually everything else: by reading.

There were other factors that made that night at Vertigo Books a fortuitous point of origin for my rebirth as a punk. Up until then, sports had been a central part of my identity and, outside of reading, had been the dominant pastime of my extracurricular life. At various times I'd juggled soccer, karate, baseball, basketball, wrestling, and track, but the grisly destruction of my lower left leg had cast a pall over my future as a multisport athlete. A few weeks prior, I'd fractured my leg for the second time in two weeks while playing in the championship game of Montgomery Soccer Institute's Boys Division 1 Under-14 Select league. I never determined exactly when the first leg injury occurred, but I compounded the damage by ignoring it. Dismissing the first fracture as some kind of unusually stubborn muscle soreness, I'd avoided the emergency room and continued to attend practice and games for about ten days while trying to hide the bum wheel from the wary eyes of my coach. By the scale of my prepubescent world, there was a lot at stake.

Our team was finally tied for first place in the elite conference we'd battled in for years. Succumbing to the persistent searing pain in my left leg would mean riding the pine during the tie-breaking final game of the season, and if that wasn't enough, I was in the midst of defending my title as the ninety-pound weight class wrestling champion in a tournament at my middle school. I managed to defeat the first-round challenger on the mats that week in school, but by the time the weekend's soccer game rolled around, my leg was more ornamental than functional.

Using some numbing muscle cream and exaggerating my gangster lean to disguise my handicap, I convinced my reluctant coach to put me in the championship match that Saturday. Within ten minutes of play, I'd overcommitted on a slide tackle and snapped the already gimpy leg, and this time I knew it. That night in the ER, doctors explained that I suffered not one but two cracks beneath the knee in the leg I'd been favoring for almost two weeks. Some orderly went out of his way to administer extensive finger wagging about how I could have saved myself considerable recovery time if I had just listened to my body and sat down at the first sign of trouble.

It was all the Black Momba needed to hear.

"After this, you ain't playing anything more strenuous than chess," she huffed in the examining room, arms akimbo and worry lines crinkling her still-youthful brown face.

Standing all of four feet eleven, ninety pounds, I was injured often enough that these emergency room trips were near routine, but this was the most debilitating setback I'd suffered yet. High school was on the horizon and our parents urged me to take stock of how much further I could truly envision myself going with sports. I was a tenacious, competitive kid who relished the thrill of a high-pressure athletic contest, and the prospect of being robbed of an outlet for all that rambunctious energy was sobering. I didn't know it yet, but the emptiness I felt when anticipating a future without sports was a void I was destined to fill with rock 'n' roll.

The leg, we were told, would take between six and eight weeks to heal completely. Since I attended a magnet school, rather than the school in the district where I lived, I took two buses to get there every morning, and our family didn't own a car. The Black Momba didn't relish a scenario in which I lugged my bulging backpack on crutches to one bus stop, settled on to the overcrowded shuttle bus, alighted at a second bus stop, rinsed, and repeated. She made the heroic move of talking Montgomery County Public Schools into sending a tutor to our house to keep me relatively up to speed with my classes for the duration of my recovery. The additional time around the house provided me, a pensive youngster to begin with, an opportunity for introspection that streamlined a teenage self-reinvention. Sitting out from school for the duration of a grading period was such a jarring breach of the rhythm I'd established as a student, I was already beginning to think of the injury as having divided my life into distinct "before" and "after" sequences. That the latter was an utter tabula rasa both thrilled and intimidated me.

As fate would have it, the book party at Vertigo occurred during my extended recovery break from school. The festivities celebrating the release of *Step into a World* began to percolate after I'd taken in about twenty pages of O'Hara's book. While indie bookstore regulars streamed in in droves, I dog-eared a page and hobbled back to our father's side to welcome the event's attendees—many of whom were Baba's friends and colleagues. But I quickly grew tired of fielding questions about how I sustained my visible injury and grinning blandly at remarks about how much I'd grown. My head was elsewhere. I dismissed myself and pogoed around the perimeter of the store on my crutches, thinking about the punk-affiliated terms I'd just been introduced to, like DIY (Do-It-Yourself) and PMA (Positive Mental Attitude). The full import of the book and the significance of punk was still embryonic for me of course, but I had the distinct sensation that something transformative was gaining steam. One chapter in O'Hara's book briefly entertained the possibility that punk could burn out on its own nihilism, and the notion would later serve as the inspiration for the name of the laughably terrible, very first punk band I ever played in: Burned Out Nihilism. Behind the exuberant music, the confrontational hair, and fashion choices, there was a spirit that animated punk to which I felt incontrovertibly native. I felt not that I was discovering something to aspire to become but rather that I was finally supplied with a word for something I'd always been. While Baba and Kevin were busy holding court and signing copies, I slipped *The Philosophy of Punk* into a stack of books

Baba had set aside for purchase from Vertigo, and my new gateway drug came home with us that night.

○ ○ ○ ○

Growing up in our hyperliterate household, Gyasi, I was predisposed to be a bit incredulous of the standard middle school English teacher trick of using pop music lyrics to make poetry accessible to skeptical youth. I resented the assumption that I, merely by virtue of being a teenager, would turn my nose up at unaccompanied verse. It seemed like an indictment to conclude that the only way I could grasp the subtle art of arranging words thoughtfully was through an exegesis of a Top 40 song. Condescension notwithstanding, the turning point in my exposure to punk lyrics is largely indebted to my eighth-grade teacher. As part of our summer reading assignment, my classmates and I were asked to find and analyze five poems, but we were permitted to substitute two songs for two of the poems. Most of the kids in my class made unimaginative selections—your predictable Robert Frost and Emily Dickinson staples—but one pimply kid in a padlock necklace and Vans sneakers brought in two texts that blew my mind.

Ryan was, more or less, the magnet program's token punk. He was rarely seen without a graphic print T-shirt advertising one of various Fat Wreck Chords bands, and his greasy brown hair was gelled vertically in something of a diet mohawk. Just two years earlier in the sixth grade, Ryan had worn thick glasses and demonstrated a dogged commitment to polo shirts. He also had a habit of compulsively brushing aside the curtains of his mushroom haircut while bragging incessantly about his accomplishments on the youth tennis circuit. He was either indifferent or oblivious as copious flecks of spit scattered from his chapped lips and landed on your face. Ryan's personality in his punk rock incarnation was as awful as his erstwhile country club persona, but I recognized that his adoption of the edgy skateboarder look was a direly needed spoonful of sugar to help the lousy medicine go down.

We ended up in the same group for the poetry assignment. Ryan had chosen to analyze Operation Ivy's "Room without a Window" and "Big City." If I had heard recordings of the two songs before reading the lyrics, I'm not sure they would have made the same impact. When Ryan later played me the tracks on his Discman, the band's upstrokes, heavily stylized vocals, and scrappy production value grated my nerves on first listen. But just as *The Philosophy of Punk* proselytized me so successfully, being introduced to Operation Ivy in a literary context made me more receptive to the punk gospel. In eighth grade I was an avowed fan of groups like Public Enemy and Rage Against the Machine, which meant I was no stranger to vague sloganizing passed off as political songwriting. Yet there was something about Operation Ivy's razor-sharp social critique that transcended mere agitprop. For starters, "Big City" and "Room Without a Window" sang unaccompanied on the page like literature, despite being written to be warbled into feedbacking PA systems at ramshackle Bay Area punk clubs. Frontman Jesse Michaels is a deviously clever lyricist, and his adroitness with imagery and metaphor enable the band's aggressive, hard-edged ska punk to communicate youthful disaffection intellectually as well as viscerally.

Around the time I was introduced to Operation Ivy, I happened to catch an episode of MTV's *Fanatic* about a thirty something computer programmer who worshipped metal-rap meatheads Limp Bizkit. That episode's titular figure wore a Limp Bizkit T-shirt beneath his work clothes every day to remind himself of his true priorities and passions in life. On the outside he was a corporate shill, but an avatar of his highest self lurked beneath the uniform he grudgingly wore to make a living. Operation Ivy is neither a stylistic nor ideological compatriot of Limp Bizkit, but I found the ritual apt and would go on to spend shifts at countless day jobs with my Operation Ivy merch in tow as a talisman.

The central conceit of "Room Without a Window" compares American society to a barren, viewless chamber constructed on the backs of the suffering poor and painted over in palatable hues with religious and political rhetoric. The tone of the song was unquestionably didactic, but Michaels's rhetorical approach nimbly sidestepped my antiauthoritarian defenses. I especially appreciated how the speaker in "Room Without a Window" announced himself as a dispassionate observer, speaking to his audience as if they were equals.

In "Big City," Michaels takes on income inequality in urban spaces with equal aplomb, memorably capturing the ambivalence of someone acutely aware of capitalism's odiousness but nonetheless nestled firmly in its thrall.

I came at poetry, and to a great degree pop music lyrics, with a particular critical lens because of the conversations that were a daily component of the ambience back home at Asim HQ. In my and Joe's early childhood, Baba was the anchor member of a performance poetry collective called So What? Joe and I grew up in the laps of the troupe's five other members, attending enough performances to commit their set to memory. While So What? took the stage, Joe and I would set up shop in the back of the audience and mimic every physical gesture and lip-synch every rhyme, a pair of pseudo-cultured ventriloquist dummies. Despite his participation, Baba was skeptical of the whole performance poetry aesthetic. He mentioned often that blustery emotionalism couldn't save a poem, that the best work didn't rely on impassioned recitation as a crutch because the poem should "stand up on the page."

With a writer for a father and a playwright as a mother, I was admittedly a tough crowd, but as I watched Ryan gesture at the band's lyrics on the classroom overhead projector, I suspected I'd finally stumbled upon a band amounting to more than screeched platitudes. That evening, I fired up the household desktop and dialed into the primitive interweb to prowl for mentions of Operation Ivy. Within an evening or two, I'd absorbed the band's lingo, origin story, and rhetoric the way many kids memorized batting averages or comic book canon.

Earlier that school year, I'd also had a passing conversation with our father that, unbeknownst to him, had nudged me toward the advent of my punk rock identity.

"I'm thinking about getting a haircut," I said to my father in the kitchen one day.

"Really?" Baba asked, raising an eyebrow. "As in, you're going to cut it all off?"

At the time, I toggled between rocking a giant bird's nest of an Afro with the sides shaved and densely situated twists you might mistake for locks. It was the late 1990s, and dreadlocks were not yet a choice that the cultural mainstream smiled upon. Dreads still generated scowls of disapproval and conjured associations with chronic joblessness, body odor, and marijuana. In general, "natural hair," as unprocessed, extension-free black hair is often called, was not as common or celebrated among black folks of the day, to say nothing of the bizarre mix of revulsion and perverse fascination it often induced in white folks.

"I'm thinking about wearing short hair now," I explained, running my hand absently through the labyrinthine curls that dangled haphazardly from my head. Aaron McGruder's seminal comic strip *The Boondocks* was beginning to make national waves that year, and a black girl in my math class had taken to calling me "Huey" on account of the similarity between my feral 'fro and the one the strip's protagonist wore. "I could go for the more clean-cut look."

My father made a noise. His disappointment was palpable, but he wouldn't deign to be completely transparent about it.

"Why now?" he asked, his tone casual.

I'd been growing my hair long since fifth grade and mostly enjoyed sporting a do that encouraged furtive rubbernecking and the occasional outright derision from my classmates. I hadn't discovered punk yet but already delighted in antagonizing pious normies for sport. As hormones took over, however, I started to wonder if all the iconoclasm was too strong a deterrent to the opposite sex.

"Some girls in my grade have been telling me I'd be much more attractive with a conventional cut," I confessed. I pictured my face framed by the sharp angles of a Caesar number 2. I daydreamed about how the neat symmetry and elegant contours of the high and tight hairstyle would flatter features currently underserved by my more idiosyncratic look.

Baba was silent. Clearly my motives were unpersuasive.

"I don't know, what do you think, Baba?"

His back was toward me as he dried a stack of dishes and filed them away in a cabinet above the sink.

"I think, like Ralph Waldo Emerson wrote, that 'whoso that would be a man must be a nonconformist.'"

Baba was gone before I could stammer a response. I was familiar enough with Emerson's *Self-Reliance* to recognize the reference, but the sentiment had never sunk in with the gravity that it did in that moment. Though he'd done so with a subtlety that bordered on the passive-aggressive, I understood my father to say that capitulating to the aesthetic preferences of teenage girls amounted to cowardice. After he left the room, it occurred to me that the question of socially acceptable hairstyles might have been a little close to home for him. Ten years prior, while in his late twenties, Baba had rocked dreads in North St. Louis when virtually no one in the somewhat culturally austere midwestern town was wearing them. In those days Joe had gotten in to more than a couple of fistfights instigated when someone had cracked, "That's why your father's Bob Marley!"

As a rising young journalist in the provincial Midwest, Baba had made a deliberate, pro-black political statement in resisting pressure to maintain a more anodyne appearance. He gave up his shoulder-length locks only in deference to a receding hairline—not to respectability politics. In other words, our dad's rebel bonafides were too solid to dismiss, but to his credit, he didn't drub me over the head with it. It was like he was a former college football player and I was whining that they hit too hard in Pop Warner. However brief and understated, the conversation was formative in shaping my worldview and laid the foundation to my receptivity to punk rock attitude. In my father's eyes, submitting to mockery and dismissal for having untamed natural hair was a concession unbecoming of a man. I would soon learn that the same behavior was frowned upon through punk's uncompromising lens as well. As much as I was eager to rebrand as a tween lothario, I was ultimately more interested in challenging a value system that placed such a premium on compliance with arbitrary social conventions. Follicles were just one front upon which to challenge the master script, but it was a battleground I wasn't willing to relinquish quite so easily.

o o o o

My earliest inkling that I was born to rock is linked to the illest Christmas present I've ever received. I was five or six years old and Grandma Joyce had bought me a Teddy Ruxpin phone. The oversized touch-tone phone toy was bright red with white buttons and a green light near the earpiece that lit up to alert you of an incoming call. If you dialed any random combination of numbers, Teddy or his mildly cantankerous sidekick, Grubby, would answer and simulate a conversation with you using a script of prerecorded questions and answers. Summers I would stretch out in the rocking chair in Grandma Smith's spare room—baby powder caked all over skinny neck to salve my chronic heat rash, knotty brown hair standing straight up on my head like an electrocuted cartoon character—and spend the better part of an hour running my mouth on the Teddy Ruxpin phone.

"Hi! This is Teddy Ruxpin!" the recording chirped with mechanical geniality.

"Hi, Teddy!" I'd play along. "What are you doing today?" Knowing the device's limited range of conversational possibilities, I made comments that teed Teddy up to spit back the boilerplate in a way that approximated an organic exchange.

"Grubby and I are going to the zoo today. What's your favorite kind of animal?"

"Sounds fun, Teddy. My favorite is a giraffe."

"Uh-huh."

"They're tall and weird-looking and their name is kind of like my name."

"What's your favorite kind of music?"

At this question, my mind always drifted back to an earlier turning point in my brief tenure on Earth: Little Richard's guest appearance on *Sesame Street*. The flamboyant showman's dazzling piano wizardry and virtuosic pipes had captivated me immediately. I didn't know if it was the androgynous appearance or the exuberant use of musical nonsense syllables or just the hypnotic speed at which his fingers colonized the keys—but something about the man and the music resonated with a part of myself I hadn't known was there. Somewhere along the way, I learned the alliterative, sing-songy phrase for what Little Richard represented, and the term felt custom fitted for my lips.

"Rock 'n' roll," I'd say in answer to Teddy Ruxpin's question, and every time it felt like I was reciting an incantation. Sure, I didn't know *exactly* what rock 'n' roll was, but I was certain I was speaking magic words.

Upon overhearing this, Joe had on more than one occasion looked up from his action figures to announce his disgust.

"Rock 'n' roll?" he spat. His arched right eyebrow formed a doppelganger of the crisply slanted part in his hi-top fade. "Ew, G'Ra! Only white people like rock music."

Joe was all of nine years old, but the implicit accusation in his words was the shape of things to come. His surprise and distaste for my musical leanings would prove to be motifs over the next twenty years. Other people's attachment to the stalest stereotypes about race and rock 'n' roll would prove astoundingly resilient and pervasive for the duration of my tenure as a creator and appreciator of rock culture. The perceived incongruity between my group membership and my aesthetic tastes became an unavoidable talking point in so many of my social experiences, from dating to auditioning for bands to writing for publications. People consistently acted like professing a deep love for rock 'n' roll while inhabiting a black casing was an aberration that demanded a scientific explanation. When I talk to adults who experienced similar stigmatization for being alt kids of color, they often indicate that it shook their sense of self. Being mocked for listening to music that was against type made them question their authenticity as ethnic people, as if appreciating only a narrow, particular set of cultural traditions was the defining criterion of their identity. I've always been troubled by this, probably because I was inclined to assume that *everyone else* was tripping when it came to rock music and prescriptive racial politics.

A simple equation led me to the patent falsity of the dominant view. My race, as I understood it, was static. The hue of my epidermis, the texture of my hair, the structure of my nose would, permanently and unequivocally, invite my categorization as black. As I saw it, this made my expertise on the subject position of blackness as unimpeachable as my appearance.

1. I was (immutably) black.
2. I loved rock music.
3. Therefore, black people can love rock music.

This stance of defiance didn't come from nowhere. As I saw it, I was taking cues from my favorite childhood comic strip. When Joe and I were in elementary school, Baba gave us a *Calvin and Hobbes* collection for Kwanzaa several years in a row. By the mid-1990s we had amassed nearly the entire history of the strip around the house. My lifelong best friend, Jonathan, often jokes that the whole of my personality is indebted to *Calvin and Hobbes* cartoonist Bill Watterson. In one of the best strips, Hobbes, the stuffed tiger who grows into a full-size yet curiously bipedal talking feline when he and Calvin are alone, asks Calvin what he's doing. When Calvin explains that he's looking for frogs, Hobbes asks how come. "I must obey the inscrutable exhortations of my soul," he tells Hobbes. It was a sentence that sent me rushing to the dictionary, a code that once cracked, dappled my inner landscape for good. The imperatives of the self—often enigmatic if they're even knowable—are nonetheless holy. To heed them is to court the company of the gods. Calvin's quip makes no mention of race, but I came to view the idea as especially consequential for black people. If Du Bois made a mission of affirming that we have souls, then that sanctity extends to the inscrutable exhortations they make of us.

That friends, family members, authority figures, and mass media insisted that this reasoning was flawed only meant that I had no choice but to constantly confront my racial identity while exploring my rock 'n' roll one. The pressure to revise my tastes so they better corresponded with my appearance hipped me to the adhesiveness of stereotypes, to the durability of the illusion that any group of people are monolithic. But then, subverting people's expectations just by being myself was nothing new to me—which is part of what attracted me to punk to begin with. Between being raised in a poor, black, bohemian family of quixotic values and answering to an ambiguously ethnic, unpronounceable name, I felt keenly an irreducible otherness that I thought would always exclude me from the normative ideals of society. At times, this sense of illegibility was frustrating, isolating, even depressing. Most often, however, it was pretty fucking punk rock.

One late winter night I am seated in Insomnia Cookies, a joint near my graduate school campus that profits by exploiting the untimely cravings of sleepless students. To my left sits an attractive woman of thirty years named Angie, a fellow graduate student who is pursuing a master's in philosophy and education. Hours before, we spent the evening in a campus library discussing her coursework. She enumerated her doubts about Hegel, waxed rhapsodic about Thoreau, and pushed back against Arendt as I sat in rapt attention, neglecting schoolwork of my own that had been the pretext for my presence there. Angie wasn't namedropping to impress me and there was nothing pedantic about her off-the-cuff musings. She was preoccupied with these subjects in a manner that was refreshingly organic. In between bites of warm chocolate chunk cookie, Angie wants to know about my name.

"I like it, but it's so unusual," she marvels, her words muffled behind the veil of shapely fingers she presses to her lips to hold cookie crumbs at bay. A few stray ones revolt and careen into my lap anyway. "How did you get it?"

"I was named for a poet," I explain. "The original G'Ra was a jazz performance poet from Chicago that my parents liked in college. At a reading once he told my pops it meant 'glory of the sun,' and the way my mom tells it, my dad knew right away that he wanted to name a child after the guy."

My date tells me that she goes by Angie among her friends and classmates, but she has three additional names that reflect her heritage. She is Chinese on her father's side and Vietnamese on her mother's. When translated into English, her three non-Anglo names form a lovely and mysterious sentiment: "beautiful moon history."

"That's so dope. 'Beautiful moon history' totally sounds like an Allen Ginsberg metaphor," I quip, and Angie laughs knowingly.

Suddenly we've appropriated the tropes of romance movies, dissolved into that tidy, mutual-smiling-without-speaking thing that signals the blossoming of amorous subtext into palpable *bow-chicka-wow-wow*. My eyes are tracing a constellation of fetching freckles across the smooth cosmos of her cheekbones when a song I loved in high school comes on the radio.

"Oh dip, this is my jam!" I shout, loud enough for every cookie junkie in the vicinity to hear. The tune in question is approaching fifteen years old and was never a single. It is a rare gift of the usually harsh and mercurial radio gods that this particular teenage anthem has converged with this moment. Taking Back Sunday's sweet-and-sour vocal tandem,

Adam Lazzara and John Nolan, trade histrionic, major-key yelps and growls over a skittery backbeat as I mouth every word. Impassioned lip-synching, however, is inadequate to convey my enthusiasm. What with the peaking attraction between my date and me, I'm already in a good mood, but now I really need to get wicked. Much to my companion's amusement, I stand up from my stool and contort my limbs quasi-rhythmically in a crude approximation of pop locking. My shoulders gyrate as if I'm shivering from cold.

"Whoa, this is so weird," Angie murmurs, mostly talking to herself. "You're dancing like you're black."

Nooooooooooo! an internal voice despairs, drawing out the syllable like a Spanish-language soccer broadcaster announcing a goal. *It was going so well, too!*

The rational part of me immediately knows where this is headed. Her two lone sentences are an ominous dorsal fin lurking in opaque surf; I've seen enough to be assured of the existence of a depressingly stupid set of racialized assumptions underneath. From prior experience I know that this is, by itself, reason enough to leave the beach, but for some reason I don't. Instead, I offer a wan half smile, half grimace and hope she'll leave it alone.

She doesn't.

"Oh my god, so this is like a thing with you," Angie says, peering at me almost clinically, as if I am some evolutionary anomaly she would like to examine on a petri dish. "You like this white boy music but you're dancing like you're black."

I try not to hear her, hope I can distract myself with the song's piano-driven bridge. But I can't concentrate. She's talking over nearly the best part. John Nolan is about to sing the bridge a glottis-tearing octave higher than he did the first time, and ya girl is absolutely ruining it. Maybe I can nip this in the bud with a quickness.

"Look, I don't really want to get into it," I begin hesitantly, "but this is a perspective that people have used to denigrate me almost my entire life. Literally since I was in like middle school."

Angie just smirks.

"I've heard this a billion times," I grumble, admittedly losing patience. "And I think it's pathetic, ignorant, and destructive."

"It was just a joke," Angie swears. Her eyes are twinkling, as if this is some cute misunderstanding, part and parcel with the witty repartee that has carried us through the night up until about ninety seconds ago. "I really didn't mean to offend you."

Her eagerness to minimize the misstep irritates me even more.

"It might not seem like a big deal to you," I go on, "but the idea that blackness is a fixed identity from which anyone with brown skin can never deviate is an oppressive thing that hurts actual people. I would know."

"I guess I just have to get used to you being—I guess—*sensitive* about that kind of thing," Angie sighed. "Because I make jokes like that with my friends in California all the time. It's really diverse there and so we're all comfortable with that kind of humor."

At about this time I start thinking about an exasperating trend in people's reactions when someone commits a racial faux pas. Often, the impulse is to dismiss the transgressor as well-meaning but merely uninformed, and certainly not representative of a broader societal pattern or anything. Impolitic utterances come from a place of ignorance rather than malice, it is commonly alleged, and "educated" people know better than to traffic in rash generalizations. These are all attractive delusions I do not presently have the luxury of succumbing to. I had purposely sought out one of the most informed women I could possibly find, on a campus at a world-class institution, and she was thwarting our burgeoning romance with the sort of reckless stereotyping that, as Obama Age conventional wisdom would have it, a highly cultivated mind like hers would dismiss out of hand. As you know, I'm not one for assuming congruence, solidarity, or symmetry between black people and other people of color who aren't black, but Angie is a person of color herself. She had lived on three different continents, studied Buddhism in a monastery, and was fluent in multiple languages—but a black kid from the hood with a soft spot for Long Island mainstreamo classics crashed the server of her imagination. We would go on to recover from the snafu for the evening, but the incident revealed a divide that would contribute to our eventual undoing.

It was a slight variation on the theme, an illustration of the ways punkness and blackness secretly affirm one another. Precisely because you are someone who stands at the particular intersections that add up to our shared social location, I want to account for how I have embraced punk rock not as a refutation but as a transvaluation of my blackness. Blackness and punkness have played out in my life as contrapuntal melodies that, if one were to listen to them independently, would seem to clash, but when heard together form a resounding chorus.

In the five years since Freddie Gray's death, when the nexus between the Black Lives Matter movement and punk rock attitude began to shimmer into my conscious view, the synergy between resisting social injustice and defying our cultural pigeonholes has entered a golden age. Entities celebrating and amplifying black punk culture—like Punk Black, AfroPunk, Decolonise Fest, Break Free Fest, and others— have spiked in stature and activity. Each of these platforms makes a point of upping the social justice ante at the same time they're upping the punx. A gate that was so recently sentineled now swings wide open. Nowadays it's far less unusual to slam dance in pits where whirling dreadlocks, twists, and box braids form a kinky canopy or to crowd surf over seas of outstretched, exclusively brown arms.

Gyasi, I don't mean to subscribe to any retract-the-ladder-behind-me school of punk. It's genuinely thrilling to me that black people are increasingly permitted to like what they like at no cost to their self-concepts. But I'd be lying if I didn't acknowledge that I have benefited from infiltrating this subculture at a time when my presence was by and large treated as some baffling aporia. Principally, the experience showed me the same thing I hope to impress upon you—that permission to fully inhabit our humanity isn't something we need to ask anyone for. It is our birthright. When you dare to live wholly in your humanness—to extend luxuriantly into its every crack and corner—you will likely discover that every seemingly unified front conceals a few defectors-in-waiting. Should you find yourself shouted down by a majority, their unanimity is an illusion more often than not. Provided that you're willing to get it started, there are those who will about-face and join you in the mosh pit or the march.

Ace Up My Sleeve

An Annotation of the Matches'
"More Than Local Boys"

Fluorescent lights flicker and glow in time to the thump of Rory's bass. Jase's voice soars commandingly over the house mix as Kenny strikes the skins like they put his mother on the wrong end of a biting snap. I am perched theatrically on the precipice of the drum riser on stage left, sweating and swaying and conjuring fire from the uppermost regions of my fretboard. A densely packed crowd of about seventy people bobs affably before us, gasping in awe as Kenny twirls his sticks between exuberant drum fills. They shriek and squeal as Greg launches his guitar in dizzying circles around his neck before catching it and punctuating the maneuver with a jaunty pinch harmonic.

Near the bar in the center of the club, I can make out the silhouettes of my coworkers Special Sauce and Han, who raise their glasses and point wobbly, drunken fingers my way when they catch me looking. Scene girls, decked out in electric-hued tanks and jangly jewelry, pack the front row and rest Converse-sneakered feet on the metal fence separating the crowd from the stage as their jealous boyfriends hug themselves tightly and feign apathy. JD, my supervisor at work, is a few paces from the stage, cupping his hands over his mouth and making catcalls, fanning himself, and pretending to faint as I leap off the drum riser and windmill a power chord.

You've been to shows like this one. The last time Some Like It Hot played Baltimore's Ottobar, you came dressed in a glittery, spray-painted T-shirt you'd designed at home—likely with Jelani and Indigo's help. During this era of our band's rise, our fans often dress up in Some Like It Hot–related attire or paint their faces before shows. The Black Momba regularly packs up her minivan to bring all three of you and various proximal latchkey kids to gigs. I peer out from the stage and give the nod to what is usually a small but vocal battalion of the only black people in the house on a given night. It is 2007, and far easier to motivate folks to support niche live music than it will be a mere three years later, in large part because the major label vanguards of the punk/emo world have penetrated the mainstream. Bands like My Chemical Romance and Paramore and Gym Class Heroes are MTV staples, and as a result their lesser-known facsimiles can persuasively market themselves as potential next big things. Punk, emo, and its most palatable offshoots enjoy a cachet in mainstream culture that EDM and hip-hop has yet to completely supplant. I have set AbsolutePunk.net as the home page on my web browser. The site, which began as a Blink-182 and MxPx fan site, has blossomed into a bustling social network for the hair gel and girl jeans set.

It is later remembered as the garish, antiquated forerunner of the only slightly less hokey Facebook, but MySpace is for the moment a dominant means of discovering music. If the minor celebrity of being in an ascending local band became an addiction for me and my four nineteen-year-old bandmates, the first hit is probably the singular thrill of clicking on some girl's MySpace profile and seeing that she's selected Some Like It Hot's signature tune "Are You Making this Magic?" as her profile song. Many of the young women who gravitate toward Some Like It Hot run DIY artist promotion companies. This means they use MySpace to signal boost a select group of bands in the local scene perceived to "have potential." Several times a month, I field queries from some enterprising MySpace user whose photos display her sporting the official scene girl uniform of tight-fitting band tees, flamboyantly colored and teased locks, and gauged ear piercings. After a brief volley of messages between our band and one of these self-styled promo gurus, the latter formalizes the business relationship by providing us with crude HTML codes for digital MySpace banners. Once the codes are activated on our own MySpace page, they announce Some Like It Hot as something like a "member of the High Five Promotions family."

No band has leveraged MySpace as a marketing tool like Fall Out Boy, a savvy Chicago foursome who have solidified themselves as the emo scene's gold standard. For instance, by repeatedly mentioning a forthcoming B-side called "I Liked You a Whole Lot Better Before You Became a MySpace Whore" in interviews, they single-handedly created the casually misogynist archetype that took the 'Space by storm. None of us are sure precisely what being one entails, but the appellation is lodged in the pop punk collective consciousness as a seductive mix of anathema and aspiration. FOB reached an echelon in which bands get invited to guest host Saturday night TV lineups on teen-oriented cable channels. Bassist-lyricist Pete Wentz is the band's breakout star. Everyone knows of the band called Fall Out Boy, but if you know any one member's name, it's Pete's. Which is why the back of the shirt you made for the previous Some Like It Hot at Ottobar show read "G'Ra vs. Pete Wentz." Beneath that heading was a checklist in which you compared Wentz's strengths with mine. You gave Wentz the edge in "hair" and "fame," but you checked the boxes next to my name for "lyrics" and "guitar." You're six years old and I am twenty. I have no expectation of catching Wentz in the hair department. Hubris makes me believe, however, that closing the notoriety gap between us is as inevitable as losing the battle I am already waging against male pattern baldness. Your homespun Some Like It Hot memorabilia crystallized a mission most would write off as impossible. And I chose to accept it.

Tonight is a critical phase of that mission. This is in no small part because of the smooth, aloof-looking man of about twenty-five who stands near the middle of the crowd.

Seeming both slightly above the fray and completely at home in the club's dim house lights, he regards the five members of my band with studied concentration, his hands buried casually in the pockets of his form-fitting black jeans. I recognize the striking bone structure, the elegant protrusion in the front of his dark mane curled skyward like an apostrophe, his loping stride from countless music videos and magazine covers. He is Ace Enders, former frontman of the Early November. TEN is not quite Fall Out Boy's peer, but the band is nonetheless a heavyweight in its own right. Now a solo artist, Ace is the headliner for whom we are opening the show. He is also the founder, owner, and fledgling producer at Pink Space Studios, a recording facility he built himself so that he could begin a second career in recording promising young bands at his home in New Jersey. He is a gatekeeper at the summit of a rock 'n' roll mountaintop I have devoted myself to scaling since bypassing college two years earlier.

He is a vision of eternal grace.

"Ever so sweet," I whisper to Rory, making a pun on the title of the slow-burning make-out anthem from the Early November's 2003 full-length debut. "Can you believe Ace fucking Enders is watching us?"

His eyes light up in agreement. "Dude," he exults. It is a syllable that encompasses everything about the moment.

Kenny leads us in with a showy piece of rapid-fire stick work and Some Like it Hot segues into the bright and buoyant instrumental that makes up the first thirty seconds of our set opener. Jase squeezes his eyes shut tightly and cradles the

mic stand, crooning the lyrics I wrote with a convincing approximation of sincerity.

> *Ladies and Gentlemen:*
> *Welcome, all aboard our good ship*
> *By this beat's accord shake those hips*
> *And get in while the getting's good*
> *'Cause when the getting's gone you'll wish you would*
> *Have participated in this courtship*
> *Please make no mistake the dance floor is*
> *Dolled up in their Sunday best for this*
> *And sweating to a drop-your-dress chorus.*

I chance another look at Ace's face in the crowd. A grin
has usurped the blue steel expression he sported a few moments before. His stylized cowlick is now flailing in time to the
music. You'd have to know just how many fortune cookies I'd
handed out in the eighteen months prior to understand how
much is riding on this moment.

o o o o

"Look on my work ye mighty, and despair," I mutter to myself while twirling a circular plastic serving tray on my finger
like a second-rate Harlem Globetrotter. "Like really, despair.
Definitely despair."

It's three weeks before the gig opening up for Ace Enders,
and I'm at work, squirming in the grip of the purgatorial vo-
cation sometimes called waiting tables at P. F. Chang's. The

nascent dinner rush is developing steadily and, because it's Thursday, likely to peak around eight o'clock. The pre-rush stillness has for the moment, however, afforded me the luxury of having only two tables, so I'm actually doing a lot more griping about the *prospect* of working than working. Each of my tables has just gotten their bland and overpriced food, so I saunter off to the bathroom to indulge my narcissism and triple-check my appearance in case of the marginal possibility that an unaccompanied cute girl sits in my section.

As I am giving myself a once-over, my good friend and colleague Han emerges from the adjacent stall.

"Dog, I just took the meanest shit!" he crows, pinching his nose and fanning himself like a fat black woman at Sunday service. "That shit was so mean, when it came out, it looked up at me and said 'Fuck you, nigga!'"

I have to laugh, having long since given up chiding Han on the civic irresponsibility of N-word usage. Many would hesitate to accept the term from the perpetually smirking lips of a five foot five, half Chinese, half Vietnamese cat like Han, but social rules be damned—I love this dude.

"Hey, man, you should be grateful. Means your metabolism is in good shape," I tell him. He sidles up next to me in front of the mirror, acquiesces to his own considerable vanity.

"Maybe it is, son. But my pockets are in worse shape. I need to make some money tonight bad, son."

We exit the bathroom slowly, both reluctant to get back to the trenches. Han's gaudily gangster limp strikes me, not for the first time, as so well-appropriated that he is almost a parody of himself; he is somehow Tina Fey to his own Sarah Palin, simultaneously Rick James and Dave Chappelle.

We're rounding a corner into the kitchen when a manager accosts us.

"Alright, guys, let's bring it in for a pre-shift," the squat man in a sloppily ironed black suit is saying. Our fellow servers scramble to the kitchen to humor him. Every full-time P. F. Chang's serf among us could deliver this speech from memory.

About this time every shift, the monotony plunges my right brain into the same cognitive amalgam of *Tetris* and *Scrabble*, and I am transfixed by the stubborn clatter of syllabic round pegs against square melodic holes, the pressure and force occasionally yielding a lyrical diamond.

> *A tank full of gas and a pocket full of cash*
> *Ain't worth the price I know*
> *Of wasting my life at bus stops and red lights*
> *To get places I don't even want to go*

I am not always so lucky, but today inspiration is an expert vandal. It tags my memory indelibly and melts away without a trace. Pedestrian demands reappear as suddenly as if I'd blinked.

"Let's remember what our goals for tonight's shift are, ladies and gentlemen. Focus on merchandizing the menu, selling wine flights, and maintaining a good timing and tempo," the squat man drones. After that, what I know to be a crisp, authoritative voice is reduced to a tonal quality most immediately comparable to the voices of Charlie Brown's parents, and as much as I'd like to think this is my highly subjective interpretation, the fourteen pairs of glazed-over pupils around me suggest otherwise.

The blathering figurehead before us is JD, my friend and incongruously also my boss. He is the kind of exhorter you'd expect to give a rousing half-time speech in a seminal sports movie, but this destiny has eluded him and he instead manages an Americanized Chinese food restaurant at the mall. A blend of locker room gumption and double-overtime gravitas informs his tersely delivered instructions on the restaurant floor.

I am not keen on hearing these particular instructions at the present time, however, and sass dribbles out of my mouth before I can stop it:

"JD, if I may interject here, you think maybe we could segregate this pre-shift by skill level, public high school style? We could have like an 'on-level' pre-shift for those of us who have not fully internalized the importance of wine flight sales and a 'gifted and talented' pre-shift for the veterans here who are already well-versed in the hallmarks of quality P. F. Chang's food service."

A mild round of titters and guffaws trickles from the circle of servers. He is cocking an eyebrow warily at me, probably buying time to conceive a witty retort of his own.

"And where would you personally fit into this scheme?" he's asking. "You didn't mention a remedial level."

"Burn!" Han yells stupidly. The jeering this induces is half-hearted. The pre-shift ends and the crew heads off toward (allegedly) more important matters.

"Walk with me," JD barks at me as he paces purposefully out of the kitchen and into the dining room. I fall into step behind him, eyeballing my tables to anticipate any possible needs I might be badgered into tending to while I'm at it. "I came so fucking close to fucking the new bitch Michelle last night," JD tells me breathlessly out of the corner of his mouth. "It was just me and her in the office at the end of my closing shift, yo. The bitch had come in to eat and drop off an application and she had this sexy ass dress on." I am straining to hear him over the buzz of the now nearly full dining room when the other manager on duty waddles past.

"What's happenin,' playas? We got two good men on this shift at least," he hollers at JD and me before dapping us up. The thirtysomething P. F. Chang's lifer and Operating Partner rocks a shaved head and a gelatinous waistline. He looks kind of like how Gordon from *Sesame Street* might look if he were bespectacled—not quite as children's-television-handsome and a bigger fan of pork rinds. He is the only black manager around and would like to make sure you never forget it. "Y'all catch that Tyler Perry movie on TBS last night?" Soulful Manager bellows. "That joint was bangin'!"

Because of Soulful Manager's proximity, JD reflexively changes the tone of our conversation without missing a beat.

"So I'm going to need you to keep an eye out for the servers in the sections in front of and behind you because we're really going to need to emphasize teamwork tonight," JD chides me, the cadence of his voice now entirely different from the porno narration style he had adopted moments ago. "We'll probably go on at least a half hour wait tonight, so when turning your tables over, keep in mind . . ."

Soulful Manager strides jovially away in a direction opposite ours, probably to argue with Han over which video has earned their vote for tonight's installment of *Rap City: The Basement*. As quickly as you could tap the "back" button on any Internet browser, JD reverts to dorm room bull session mode. He leans in to me conspicuously, and my air space is awash in cologne that smells expensive but probably isn't.

"And I'm thinking about how bad I really wanna fuck her right there in the office, yo, but I know I don't have a condom on me for one, and on top of that, if I'm gonna fuck a bitch like Michelle, yo, I'm gonna have to do a good job."

We've arrived at the front of the restaurant, a few feet outside of my section and just a stride or two from the host stand.

"Hi, there," a schoolmarmish patron cuts in, clearly aware that she is interrupting something. "I was hoping to speak to a manager about my experience here tonight. Is one available?" The thinly veiled annoyance in her voice is palpable, and while hearing her talk encourages me to thank Zeus that she's not my mom, I feel sorry for this lady, and not because of the booger she found in her shrimp dumplings—or whatever she's in the process of launching a complaint about.

JD may be a bit of a butterball, but his handsome baby face and an uncanny ability to go from urban to urbane in six-tenths of a second make him a social juggernaut.

It's like watching Optimus Prime emerge from what was a common fire truck only seconds ago. His excessive usage of "yo" morphs into a barrage of "ma'ams" and "beg your pardons" that stifle Soccer Mom's stammered rebuttals like a phalanx of beaten Decepticons. I don't need to watch the rest of the scene unfold to anticipate how it ends: the once-disgruntled patron leaves happy with a comp card in hand and an intention to grace us with her repeat business as JD swaggers away, dusting his hands off before disappearing to the back of the restaurant to rhapsodize about Michelle's breasts to the next convenient ear.

A new table is seated in my section. I retreat to the kitchen to produce a trio—a tray of sauces that P. F. Chang's proto-col demands I present to the table upon greeting them. Part of the schtick is that I use the trio to create a savory "special sauce" to complement my table's meal.

The occupants of my newest table—or "guests" as we're trained to call them—look like they're on a short dinner re-cess from a Republican National Committee meeting. The three older, comb-over-sporting white dudes before me look bored before I have even begun talking.

"Good evening, gentlemen. Thanks for waiting and wel-come to P. F. Chang's Bistro." I tell them my name, which is always a hurdle, so I follow it up with this:

"I'm the Jackie Robinson of modern P. F. Chang's table service, so if you forget my name, I still probably won't be too tough to identify should you need to describe me to a colleague."

I am not sure if the silence that follows—so intense that I can actually hear the flames licking at the decorative candle at the center of the table—is a specific reaction to my acknowledgment of being the only black server on the floor or just the turnaround time required for the geezers' slowed synaptic response. Eventually the boldest of the RNC members speaks up.

"OK, we'll have the chicken lettuce wrap to start, and I'll have an iced tea."

The RNC leader's choice of beverage starts a trend, and his company follows his lead, lemming-like.

"And I think I'll have an iced tea, too."

"Gimme one also."

"Right away, gentlemen. But before I get that started for you, I'm going to mix up our patented special sauce in case you'd like to add a little flair to your appetizers or entrées." Here, of course, is when I throw in the definitive mark of the P. F. Chang's brand: the highly touted brainchild of our top corporate marketing strategists. I assume the precision of a surgeon as I indiscriminately mix the four sauces that make up the trio. I even make a show of pausing thoughtfully like a pioneering chemist before stirring the resultant goo conclusively and blurting "That should do it for ya."

In theory, the concoction of special sauce should personalize the experience for guests. It should highlight the server's direct contribution to the enhancement of their meal. But most of us make the sauce with about the same amount of forethought we put into finger painting in preschool. The fact that a bunch of marketing gurus with MBAs from Harvard Business School have decided this is a concept to build a franchise around is unfathomable—and hilarious—to me.

As I'm punching the new order in, Soulful Manager is introducing everyone on the staff to a new trainee. Han is already spitting game at her.

"Everybody, we have a new face in the building," Soulful Manager announces to the front-of-house employees in the kitchen. "Her name is Michelle, but I'm gon' call her Lil' Momma. Say 'what's up' to Lil' Momma if you get a chance today."

"Baby, lemme offer you a warm welcome to P. F. Chang's China Bistro," Han says to the latest object of JD's testicular fascination in a way that suggests, in his head at least, his voice comes out like Barry White's.

Michelle giggles shyly. "Thank you."

He stoops to his knees, outstretches her arm, and kisses her hand tenderly. This appears to have emboldened her, because she's now comfortable enough with Han to say this:

"Oh my God—do you remember the rapper Jin? Like from Ruff Ryders. Eve and DMX and all them?"

Han studies her face, still kneeling and holding her hand to his lips.

"Word? You fuck with Ruff Ryders, shorty?"

"You kinda look like him. Like Jin, I mean."

Han releases her hand, stands.

"Oh. Well, you ever heard of the actress joint Charlize Theron?"

Michelle giggles some more, eager to be "flattered" in return. "Yeah, I love her!"

"Yeah, um, you *don't* look like her."

She doesn't, but that's immaterial in the relentlessly lascivious world of server culture. Out of the corner of my eye I can see JD and several other waiters leering in Michelle's general direction.

"I'm just playing with you, shorty," Han reassures Michelle, laughing and clapping her on the back. "You alright. Did you meet my man yet?" He gestures to me, and Michelle and I shake hands. "He's in a band. He plays guitar, writes songs, he's on that rock star shit." Han loves to mock me for some reason, maybe because his volunteering of my biography usually puts me on the spot. Michelle is either intrigued or being very polite.

"That's so awesome! You play bass in a band? What kind of music? Is it anything like Coldplay or Snow Patrol?"

"Um, well, no, six-string guitar, actually."

"Oh yeah. Really chill," Michelle gushes.

"And it's got more of a punk or alternative sensibility to it similar to Eve 6, sort of in the tradition of Jawbreaker—"

"I really love Coldplay, though. Chris Martin is amazing live."

I think he's kind of a bozo, actually.

"You should watch him, honestly," Michelle goes. "Like he could give you notes."

I want to tell her that her condescension is unwarranted. I mean, come on—Some Like It Hot is backed by such august institutions as 98 Rock's *Noise in the Basement*.

Like so many regional radio stalwarts, Baltimore's rock station has a weekly segment in which they show love to rising local bands. Like mine. Months earlier, Some Like It Hot's appearance on *Noise in the Basement* for an on-air interview with host Matt Davis was a turning point in the band's development. Matt at least appeared to take a genuine liking to us, and one of our first-ever acoustic performances occurred live on his show. We managed to nail the performance despite Greg, our guitar player, breaking a string in the middle of a song. In between the boilerplate questions about influences, crazy fan stories, and plans for the band's future, Matt played cuts from our self-produced EP *The Talk of the Town* over the air. Songs I'd written in our raggedy two-family flat in urban Baltimore—jams that were, as you might remember, crafted in between preparing your after-school snacks, teaching you how to play chess, and nagging you about math homework—were ringing out over the metropolitan area. My primitive cell phone convulsed with texts. My friends were geeking out about hearing the little pop punk band that could on the radio.

There was something different, however, about learning that we'd be played on the show on an occasion when we weren't physically present in the broadcast studio. The nationally renowned bands we grew up on were in heavy rotation on the radio; they didn't just earn a couple spins by virtue of being in the building. We jonesed for the legitimacy that would come with our songs achieving such a life of their own, that they would reach out and touch the public independently.

Or maybe we just wanted to simulate the exhilarating moment of rock 'n' roll rising action that the Matches immortalize on "More Than Local Boys."

After an auspicious radio debut, Matt Davis became our friend on MySpace and we kept in touch. One red letter afternoon, Matt wrote to let us know that a Some Like It Hot song was in the queue for the next show. I stocked up on Nesquik chocolate milk in preparation for a straight edge celebratory toast. Jase and I shared a house in Rockville, Maryland, with four other P. F. Chang's veterans. Most of them cleared their Sunday night schedules to turn on 98 Rock and support the dudes who made all that racket in their literal basement. About ten minutes before *Noise in the Basement* got underway, my singer and I gathered the bottles of Nesquik and headed outside to his car to tune in.

We didn't know where Some Like It Hot fell in the playlist, so we listened in rapt silence until Matt introduced our jam.

"Here's Rockville, Maryland's Some Like It Hot with 'Young Once.'"

Both my and Jase's mouths became O's. His eyebrows shot up. Real-time Jase was speechless as his own singing voice soared over the car speakers.

I was a misfit black kid who'd slunk listlessly through high school and forgone college entirely to play guitar and jump off of shit in bars I was not yet old enough to enter legally. At this point, my life experience had been divided equally between prosperous white environs and depleted black ones, and in each of these settings I'd felt I was merely passing through, a vagabond en route to some other elusive and enchanted destination. I had poured all that disidentification and loneliness and unbearable fucking boredom into a four-chord punk tune—and now it had been gloriously unleashed across the airwaves. Quite suddenly the void had a fissure, Gyasi. I felt certain I could stretch it into a wormhole.

As the last notes of Some Like It Hot's "Young Once" faded out, Jase and I sounded simultaneous barbaric yawps. The feeling of accomplishment was electric and, looking into Jase's eyes, I could see that the current was running through him as well. Our very atoms were charged with a frisson of possibility. The fact that we were only a few feet apart in his relatively compact two-door car wasn't the only reason I had readily felt what he was feeling. Though we'd only known each other a little over a year, we'd become incredibly close. It was a period of life uniquely conducive to the swift manufacture of intimate, competitive, symbiotic friendship. Our ambition and ego had congealed into a single gas giant, one with a gravitational pull strong enough to bend reality to its will. The realization of everything we'd both aspired to since first picking up a guitar seemed tantalizingly within reach.

"To the dream!" Jase crowed, unfastening the cap of his Nesquik. I knocked my bottle of chocolate milk against his.

"To the dream!" I shouted back. We both gulped down a swig and basked in the sugar rush.

Possessed by punk's equivalent of the Holy Ghost, Jase broke into an acapella rendition of the Matches' "More Than Local Boys," a song that describes Matches frontman Shawn Harris hearing his own band on the radio for the first time.

"We make noise," Jase crooned at the top of his sinewy smooth voice. "What else could we choose?"

I caught the Ghost too and chimed in with my own much shakier pipes.

"We're gonna be more than local boys," we sang in unison. "And SHAKE SHAKE SHAKE the dust off these shoes."

It wasn't purely a function of heartwarming serendipity that Jase and I burst into the same song. Car-less wonder that I was, I'd ridden shotgun as Jase blasted the Matches' debut record *E. Von Dahl Killed the Locals* for the better part of the last six months. The Matches were a Bay Area punk outfit who managed to strike an addictive balance between flexing their keen pop smarts and indulging their unrepentant weirdness. How weird, you say? Well, the summer Jase and I waited hours in the sun to catch the Matches at Warped Tour, they opened their set at the legendary skate punk festival with a string-laden waltz number. A number of Matches songs were cowritten with a mysterious, middle-aged, punk Svengali that the liner notes describe as "The Wizard" Miles Hurwitz.

E. Von Dahl's eleven tracks of restless power pop twitch with the urgency of a searingly sane person unfastening the sleeves of their own straitjacket. Out of all of them, "More Than Local Boys" is the stardom-or-bust manifesto that made two kids from Rockville believe they could imminently embody the song's title. It isn't completely far-fetched.

Some Like It Hot self-released a pair of EPs while playing monthly shows in the vibrant but brutally competitive Baltimore pop punk scene. In 2007 it's still possible to make a profit as a local band selling concert tickets and compact discs. The band has already generated a modicum of local acclaim, and with the relatively punk-friendly zeitgeist as a backdrop, our ambition to become a national act feels like no less of a pipe dream than Barack Obama's presidential campaign. Between playing paid cover sets at sweet sixteen parties and aggressively hocking merch on MySpace, the band has actually begun to pay for itself. Fans of Some Like It Hot occasionally identify Jase and me on the street in our neighborhood and stop us for pictures. Through it all, "More Than Local Boys" is the tune I play most to drown out the social clock chirping its infernal alarm while I frantically pound the snooze button.

Most of my peers from my high school class are by now juggling campus jobs, keg parties, and coursework. I'm living a life of rapid alternation between balancing merch table spreadsheets and balancing dishes of half-eaten Mongolian beef.

It comes with considerable psychological whiplash.

Like now for instance. I've wasted valuable time gabbing with Han and the newbie, and I'm not eager to find out what happens when septuagenarian right-wingers get antsy. Their drinks in hand, I'm rushing back out to the dining room floor.

"You play guitar, man?" The voice belongs to Special Sauce, a lovable, portly fellow server who I have worked with for the past three years. I nicknamed him back when we were both still bussing tables because he knows just about everything there is to know about P. F. Chang's—so much so that he embodies the quintessence of our franchise as well as our special sauce. For whatever reason, the handle stuck.

"Dude, I play, too," he announces, having eavesdropped. "I had no idea you played, man. We need to jam!"

He is the kind of drug-addled guy who would struggle to remember whether a table's order called for extra scallions or light oil but can recollect entire scenes from any stoner movie with stunning accuracy. Special Sauce's front right tooth is forever obfuscated by a thick, presumably adhesive substance that could be either cheese or peanut butter—I can never tell which—but he is glib and witty enough that you'd never be able to get a word in to call him on it.

"How is this news to you?" I ask, genuinely befuddled. "I gave you my band's demo like six months ago."

He blinks, parts his lips sheepishly to reveal that star incisor's strange graffiti.

"Oh yeah, I know. I guess I just figured you rapped or something."

I'm hoping he's joking when we're interrupted.

"Sir, could I have the check please?" The patriarch at Table 8 looks dejected as his twin youngsters, shrieking and giggling with abandon, go full Jackson Pollock on their table's surface with the sauces from the trio. He gestures at the horrific mess. "And I apologize in advance for this. They walk all over me when their mother's not around." He looks a little bit like an aging John Travolta, and I wonder if there was a time when he was a spry, leather jacket-sporting ladies' man who thought the whole wide world was his, and if that only exacerbates the pain of this neutered version that is stuck with the kids while Olivia Newton-John spends his paycheck at the mall.

My arms are full, so I have to crane my neck over the stack of glasses on my tray to tell him, "Yes, sir, I'll be right with you." At the same time, Table 7, credit card in hand, gestures wildly for my attention.

"We've got to go. We're really in kind of a rush," Table 7's business lady with a terrible weave is practically shouting. She jabs the credit card at me in a way that makes me imagine her impishly withdrawing it before cackling and yelling "gotcha!" I readjust the weight of the tray that holds the RNC drinks in my right hand while reaching for the credit card with my left. I've learned not to expect the difficulty of this maneuver to play elegantly on the heartstrings of P. F. Chang's patrons in a fashion that might foster in them even a shred of patience, but that hasn't stopped me from wishing that it would.

"Certainly, ma'am," I chirp, shoving the credit card into the front pocket of my apron. "I'm going to empty my hands and I'll run this card for you right away."

I finally arrive at my original destination of Table 6. I figure if I can drop their plates and drinks off without getting snagged taking an entrée order, I may be able to escape a potentially greasy situation with the disgruntled John Travolta lookalike and the businesswoman in an unbe-weave-able hurry. Fortunately, the Combover Club have their noses buried in their menus and don't even bother looking up when I begin unloading my tray. With the speed of a man possessed, I'm arranging plates and glasses of iced tea on the tabletop when the geezer closest to me completely pisses down my throat by saying: "Young man, I think we're ready to order now."

If this were a melodramatic television commercial or tongue-in-cheek sitcom, the long, loud, impossibly low tone indicative of foreboding would sound right after he said that.

"Absolutely, sir. Just give me one moment to—"

"Yeah, we're going to have the Chang's Chicken with a side of Szechuan asparagus," he begins, as if I've said nothing. I hastily whip out my notepad and scribble furiously, trying to keep my internal monologue from showing on my face.

"And the Mongolian beef." The geezer wheezes very slowly and deliberately as if he's talking to someone for whom

English is not a first language. Maybe the Jackie Robinson thing gave them the wrong idea.

"Make that two, actually. And we'll also have the . . ." He trails off and murmurs into the menu pages while his fingers trace the print.

I glance to my left. Disgruntled Dad at Table 8 is breaking his crazy neck looking for me, obviously eager to get his twin abstract expressionists home.

"Sir, I've really got to check in with—"

"OK. Scratch that, son. We're going to have two orders of kung pao chicken and the garlic snap peas."

"Excellent, gentlemen," I practically squeak, erasing and rewriting like my life depends on it. And it just may; a bar fight scene from *Michael* in which a winged, supernatural John Travolta lays a vicious smackdown on a group of pool hustlers is playing in my head, and I'm hoping it isn't a premonition.

"Oh, now wait a minute, Tim," says one geezer to another. "Chuck likes those chicken flatbread things. Should we get one, Chuck?"

Chuck looks thoughtful, pauses as if this is the million-dollar question in *Slumdog Millionaire* and his answer will determine whether he goes to bed with Freida Pinto every night for the rest of his life.

"Hmm, well, you know those give me heartburn sometimes. So maybe . . ."

I will phone a friend for him.

"Yeah, best to pass on that. I'll get that order started right away," and I'm gone before I can be contradicted.

The dinner rush is now in full swing and tonight's entire server roster appears to be bustling about the kitchen at once. The competition for the limited resources available to optimize our service—and to in turn maximize our tips—yields a frantic, petty mad dash that is something like capitalism incarnate. Or maybe it's like the terrifying tumult of a skirmish in 'Nam—but instead of feeling a galvanizing love and fraternity for the guy next to you, you will happily sell his ass out to ensure that your chicken lettuce wraps come out on time.

All of this is working against me as I hustle into the kitchen and embark on a panic-stricken quest to find an unused terminal, feeling much like an action hero rushing to defuse a time-sensitive hostage situation.

"Han, I'm going to need you to greet a table for Michelle," JD commands. "Make a trio and follow me."

"I've got thirty-five minutes on two entrées for Table 3!" another poor bastard hollers. There is something of an unspoken understanding among the wait staff at P. F. Chang's that one server's personal catastrophe is another's blissful oblivion. If the managers have time to help you when your table thinks you're screwing up, they will; but to the other servers, you're a Katrina refugee to their Dubya.

The surrounding madness epitomizes the trappings of maturity that I aim to transcend with just an elegant stroke of six nickel-wound strings; the Goliath I'm determined to slay in a quest that will ultimately prove the superior might of my (punk) rock. Whereas pitch-perfect customer service may elude me, rock stardom shall not.

I weave through the throng of uniformly dressed bodies when suddenly I fall into a game of musical terminals. Five servers are hurriedly en route to the four terminals that line the perimeter of the kitchen. One by one, they each notice that there aren't enough terminals to go around, but none slow their strides. I am at the wrong angle and lose out in the logjam.

"You are too sweet for waiting," coos a zaftig coworker with hypnotically glittering lips. Her hand trails titillatingly on my back as she struts out of the kitchen toward the restaurant floor, and she's gone in a cloud of some nameless but alluring perfume.

"You're telling me," I mumble to her back. "I am a nice guy who is quite literally finishing last." Travolta has appeared at the partition that separates the kitchen from the dining room. He's gesturing for the check with hyperbolic urgency, his features comically distorted through the glass.

"Just a moment, please, sir," I mouth at him while holding up one finger. He nods about eleven more times than he needs to, slaps a hand to a crinkled forehead, sighs. I step up to the terminal and print the dude's check while trying not to picture him breaking a billiards stick over my head.

I don't actually have time to make a second trip, so I call up Table 7's check also, thinking I can charge their card and still get Travolta's bill to him before he blows a gasket, but there is a problem: Table 7's credit card is nowhere to be found.

A search of my pockets comes up empty. An error like this at P. F. Chang's can be career threatening. Here comes the creep of that damning solipsism I always feel when shit hits the fan at this job. Unemployment will come first, then eviction from my sub-par apartment, homelessness soon after, and—

"Young brotha, you look like you might need some help," Soulful Manager says to me, chuckling. "What it is?"

"I've lost a credit card. I just had it like, five minutes ago," I practically moan, trying to keep the panic out of my voice. "It's a Visa."

"I'll ask everyone to look around," Soulful Manager says, his booming baritone now oddly comforting. "We gon' find that joint for ya!"

I thank him profusely, turn on my heel and bump right into Travolta on my way out of the kitchen.

"Oh, pardon me, sir, here's your—"

"Hey listen pal, I asked you for my check about fifteen minutes ago. I've got some place to be, my daughters are getting antsy, and you're back here running your mouth?" I'm holding the check out to him and he's so hot on his tirade that he's not even taking it. If JD were handy, I might have a shot at defusing this one, but things being as they are, it's not looking good.

"I apologize, sir. I haven't been running my mouth, I just have several tables to tend to—"

"And your attitude *sucks*!" he rages, finally taking the check. He shoves two twenties into the check presenter and practically throws it at me, flecks of spit glistening on each of his crimson cheeks. "You're a joke of a person, and you should be ashamed of yourself!"

It's an excellent line to leave on, and he does. There are two mitigating factors that keep me from being especially devastated about this outburst: (A) this kind of unexpected, potentially unpreventable meltdown is par for the course at P. F. Chang's, and (B) I know that I'm not yet out of the woods.

I drop down to my hands and knees and begin to retrace my steps through the kitchen. Ever since I was a kid, a part of me has believed that when you lose things, they are never actually conveniently lying somewhere out of sight, waiting to be discovered should you ever develop the presence of mind to remember precisely where you lost track of them. Instead, lost items have actually been stolen by evil Lilliputians who will hoard the items for their own dark purposes, making any frenzied searches futile. I am unsuccessfully trying to put this out of mind as Soulful Manager approaches.

"No luck with the credit card so far," he sighs. "I can let them know what happened and that we'll keep an eye out if you want me to."

His offer is generous, but not one I can accept.

"Nah, man. Thank you, though," I'm saying from the floor. "I'm going to keep looking, and if I really lost it, I'll let them know myself."

Soulful Manager nods solemnly, as if he already knows I'm a goner.

"Good man."

Soon, I've covered the limited space I had traveled with the card two times over. If I don't find it, Soulful Manager will have to give me the hook. And before long, Gyasi, you'll be making room for a third bunkmate in the double-decker bed that you and Jelani share. Suddenly I spot the credit card there, just a few inches in front of my left knee.

It's right where Han dropped it.

"Here go your card, dog," Han grumbles. "You're lucky you're my nigga or I never would've returned that shit."

However relieved, I'm speechless. In a twisted way, Han has proven my boyhood theory bizarrely accurate.

"If it was anybody else, they would be outta luck. But I couldn't fuck your shit up since we homies," Han explains further. I try out my tongue again.

"Thanks, dude. I was so scared of not finding it that I was having visions of unemployment."

"You better be lucky, dog. I could use that money so bad."

He could also do without the likely ensuing criminal record, but I don't tell him that. Instead, I run the card and return it to its owner and, as it turns out, her party wasn't in much of a hurry at all. They camp in my section for most of the rest of the night, and hook it up pretty nicely when the tip time comes, too.

At the end of the shift, my will to live has almost replenished itself when Coldplay comes over the stereo. Chris Martin and company set the mood as the handful of servers still on the clock joke around and close down the kitchen while waiting for the store's final tables to cash out and call it a night.

"There is a light in your eyes," the goofball lead singer croons, a showy falsetto adorning the last word in the line. *Come on*, I can't help but think to myself. *How long did it take him to come up with that lyric?* It's thin and platitudinal enough to make Barry Manilow cringe. I mean, is the subject of the song blinded by this light he mentioned? Is she squinting? Maybe she's at the doctor getting an eye exam and the light in question is for a medical purpose.

But even as I mock him, I realize it's probably not the lyric that sucks, but my attitude. I know that I am merely "a joke of a person," that I should be "ashamed" of myself.

My phone buzzes. Since I'm still on the clock, I fish it clandestinely from my pocket and glance at the screen. I am so thrilled with what I see that I will not delete the message for months.

Dude. I have the best news: Ace Enders from Early November listened to our demos online and he says he loves what he heard! He wants to produce us.

For the rest of the shift, there is a light in my eyes, indeed.

Mad Props to Madness

An Annotation of Bad Religion's "Pity the Dead"

In a high school English class, we were assigned a project on forms of humor. When my classmate asked me what genre my project was on, I told him black comedy.

"Oh, dude, that's legit," he said, smiling. "I love Martin Lawrence and like, Bernie Mac. Black comedians are my shit!"

I was actually writing an essay on *Rosencrantz and Guildenstern Are Dead*, an absurdist tragicomedy that didn't have any literal equivalence to something you'd see on Def Comedy Jam. My classmate's conflation of comedy authored by black people and comedy that makes light of painful or taboo experiences did hit on some kind of truth, though. "Black" modifies people in much the same way it modifies humor. It's expected that black life is to a significant degree composed of experiences we laugh at to keep from crying.

Our sister Indigo's stand-up material exemplifies this relationship. In some sets, she opens with a joke in which she mock-worries that she's sabotaging the Black Momba's career as a social justice activist by surviving all her encounters with the police. Audiences are often unsure whether to chortle or wince. I suspect you would cackle out loud unreservedly though, because it's how you were raised. Indigo has refined and perfected it and made it her own, but it's essentially the same barbed, mordant humor that the Asim siblings have been using to make each other laugh for decades.

I don't want to speak for all of us, but, in my case at least, that humor is one of the primary techniques I have used to sublimate shadows I have struggled with as far back as I can remember. Wisecracks are a trusty trojan horse for carrying lust for oblivion out of the realm of the unspeakable.

Which is what was going on that time I quipped: "If there's anything I'm looking forward to this week, it's my own destruction." We were in the kitchen of our parents' house in Massachusetts. As admissions of longing for death go, this one was at least somewhat apropos. You and I had each been reading about the imminent onslaught of Hurricane Sandy, which would in short order ravage the eastern seaboard. Classes at your middle school and my college were both canceled accordingly. You didn't really reply, but you repeated the joke and laughed, a little too heartily. I wanted to cringe. It was the first time I had consciously realized how frequently I made jokes like that to you. I wondered what it meant to be inured to such blasé discussion of death at eleven years old. Uncovering the source code behind bits of the family program feels particularly necessary now, as you form your own judgments about which heirlooms to preserve and which to discard.

As teenagers, my bookish friend Tanya and I would exchange AOL instant messages about our mutual fascination with suicide. We'd met in sixth grade as members of the incoming class of 2000 at the Eastern Middle School Humanities and Communications Magnet program, a competitive "gifted" track with a slim acceptance rate. Rejected from the counterpart program for math and science brainiacs, I had attended Eastern by default, but Tanya had been admitted to both and chose Eastern on the basis of her ambition to become an artist. Her caustic sense of humor and knack for observation made her a thrilling keypal, and I frittered away countless afternoons between seventh and twelfth grades shooting the virtual breeze with her. Each of us thought the other to be at least slightly crazy, and we admired each other for it. Certainly the vagaries of adolescent brain chemistry were a factor in our shared wariness with the world we were being groomed to inherit. But we also believed there was some nexus between being trenchant critics of a warped society and being prime candidates for eventual institutionalization.

I could never finalize a method, but I told Tanya that I'd definitely write down a single, devastating Langston Hughes line in my dismal handwriting, fold up the white piece of paper with painstaking neatness and slide it gingerly into my breast pocket before taking myself out. *The calm, cool face of the river asked me for a kiss.*[1] Tanya and I agreed that the ideal move would be to leave the line unattributed, so that it took a fellow aficionado to recognize the sentence's source: Hughes's poem titled simply "Suicide's Note." To my teenage mind, Hughes captured the perverse appeal of fleeing Earth by one's own hand. Nature's seductive placidity beckoned to me, too. Like Hughes's speaker, I often mulled the possibility that death might be more sublime escape route than grisly finale.

The line between child's play and clear and present danger blurred when Tanya actually attempted suicide when we were in ninth grade at separate schools. She'd taken enough sleeping pills to sedate New York, but her mother discovered her comatose on the bathroom floor and rushed Tanya to the hospital in time to foil her. I only learned of the near disaster a month after the fact, when she returned to AIM to give a detailed but impressionistic account of her failed exit caper.

"I'm glad you're still here," I remember tapping out once Tanya's screen name finally illuminated on my buddy list after a lengthy stint in the purgatory of the drab, colorless "offline" tab. "But I can't say I don't understand why you did it."

It probably isn't coincidence that Tanya and I were both aspiring writers, and that we traded early, fumbling attempts at prose when not trying to outdo each other's potential suicide notes. As giddy devourers of anything wordy and subversive we were influenced by the literary glamorization of madness present in the work of insurgent thinkers like Woolf, Blake, and Salinger. I realize that many people would like to conceive of mental illness as a medical condition with neat boundaries, that a person who is "crazy" can be identified as such beyond a reasonable doubt by reliable means. The history of madness as a form of social control casts any stable definition of mental illness in doubt. Tanya is just one example, but she was hardly a person out of touch with reality. She simply took a careful look around and just didn't much like what she saw. In view of Tanya's travails, and to a lesser extent, my own, I was reluctant to stigmatize those who tussled with or even succumbed to suicidal impulses. It left an imprint that a friend of such considerable promise had determined even fleetingly that this realm was not the place to be.

Tanya was a major Blink-182 fan. A number of our marathon AIM conversations were extended collaborative close readings of the lyrics to their songs. Tanya and I became friends a few short months after my punk rock awakening at Vertigo Books, at a cultural moment when Blink was an MTV darling alongside more traditional pop acts like Backstreet Boys and Britney Spears. Though I'd later come to appreciate the massively influential SoCal power trio, I regarded Operation Ivy as premium orange juice and Blink as their from concentrate counterpart. As my teens took hold and my politics took shape, I was eager for material that made sense of a disordered world. My heathen prayers were answered when Blink-182 announced a tour with their pop punk forefathers Bad Religion. I couldn't resist a band that branded themselves as the photo negative of the schlock peddled from the pulpit of our grandmother's church. Cavalierly assuming that the fact that they were sharing a bill with Blink that summer would impress Tanya, I bought the first Bad Religion compact disc I could get my hands on, 1996's *The Gray Race*. The album boasts heroic guitar solos and angelic vocal harmonies overlaid with blistering critiques of the status quo.

Tanya, it turned out, did not share my preference for punk that served as a tuneful platform for biting cultural commentary. She seemed like a lock to sympathize with the broad philosophical tilt of a band that named their first record *How Could Hell Be Any Worse?* But alas, her teenage angst was best balmed by different bards.

"I like whiny lyrics about girls," she explained. "Not crap about third-world countries." Bad Religion is no more forgiving about the deficiencies of the first. The cover art to *The Gray Race* depicts an array of listless faces staring directly at the camera, their vacant expressions and the washed out photography underscoring the spiritual vacuity of Western life. The album's lyrics enumerate all that ails this drab society aching for color and reanimation. Compositionally lean but intellectually meaty, "Pity the Dead" finds frontman Greg Graffin questioning whether the departed deserve our envy more than our sorrow. Staccato, major-key guitars and insistent cymbal work propel Graffin's unsparing summations of the dire state of the living. The perky rhythms and bright production supply an endorphin rush sunny enough to offset the dour prognosis. If the track came on shuffle mode and caught you off guard, you could have bopped along through three-quarters of it before you realized the singer was making a case that you're better off dead. "Pity the Dead" builds to a fist-pumping crescendo with Graffin advancing a heretical vision of the afterlife fitting of the band's name.

I felt vindicated to happen upon the song in the context of an album about the failings of Western civilization. It cohered with my suspicion that these irrepressible fantasies about my own demise were symptoms of being a dissident. The examined life was hard, Bad Religion seemed to be saying, and the difficult truths that emerged from that examination could make one doubt that life is worth living. Whiny lyrics about girls couldn't hold a candle.

The ambiguous line between social dissent and actual psychological malady is both a cause and effect of the extensive history of countercultural figures using craziness as a catchall symbol for objection to oppressive norms.

Encircled by a group of prepubescent boys poised to kick my ass in elementary school, I recall cheekily quoting James Brown in an attempt to deflate their confidence: "I may not know karate, but I know ka-razy." For most of my adolescence I scribbled the Operation Ivy couplet "Conditioned to self-interest with emotions locked away / If that's what they call normal, then I'd rather be insane" on any surface I could get my hands on. And in high school I blinked back tears during the conclusion of S. E. Hinton's *Rumblefish*, when Rusty James's mysterious wraith of an older brother, the Motorcycle Boy, is gunned down by the cops while appearing to rob a pet store. I saw something of myself in the brooding and understated figure who just wanted to rescue the Siamese fighting fish from captivity.

These attachments I had with the colloquial understanding of craziness made it difficult to imagine a wide gulf between mental illness and progressive nonconformity. It never seemed that implausible that I might end up a smelly, disheveled panhandler muttering to himself at a bus stop. That outcome seemed no worse than achieving what my peers set out for: the emulation of a Sitcom Dad, some bored but genial man with a briefcase, a baby, and a mortgage. Did that make me crazy? At least craziness was a breach of the normative social script, a state of not being beholden to the rules and precepts of a mainstream that didn't seem to have a place for me to begin with.

These questions resurfaced in my mind when actor-comedian Robin Williams took his own life in the summer of 2014. Williams's passing renewed collective chin-scratching about mental wellness and the ways that stigmas associated with depression can dissuade those affected from seeking treatment. A common argument held that a wealthy and widely admired person would be unlikely to succumb to hopelessness. Others countered that assuming that the rich and respected are insulated from depression reinforces the very stereotypes that make it difficult to speak candidly about the disease. So much of the lore about American individualism celebrates those who surmount adversity seemingly by way of stoic resolve alone. Of course it's hard to receive a diagnosis of emotional imbalance as something other than an indictment of one's personal fortitude.

But the mystification of mental unwellness has a social function as well. Calling people or ideas crazy is a swell way to damage the credibility of dissent. Craziness is a do-it-all tool for the dismissal of behavior that we prefer to see as extrinsic to our fundamental nature as Americans, and, more broadly, as human beings. Perceived madness is so elastic that it can be used to condemn or condone with equal success. While the suggestion that Williams battled personal demons cast the entertainer in a sympathetic light, speculations that spree shooter Elliot Rodger struggled with demons of his own cast him and the murderous rampage that cost six people their lives as anomalies wholly attributable to the misfiring of neurons. Dismissing Rodger's actions as the result of simple lunacy spares us from the discomfort of admitting that the twenty-two-year-old's chilling YouTube manifestoes are a traceable byproduct of a misogynistic and gun-obsessed cultural baseline.[2]

Dehumanizing Rodger maintains the illusion that countless otherwise "sane" people don't share his vitriol for women, minorities, and interracial couples. Making sickness the patsy elides our complicity in the maintenance of the conditions that beget sexist, racist spree shooters. Using mental illness as a scapegoat allows society to look pityingly at those who've broken up with it and conclude definitively *it's not me, it's you.* Rodger may be an aberration in the sense that his prejudices drove him to murder, but he didn't arrive at those beliefs on his own. He was a creature of a society that fomented and nurtured his narcissism, his entitlement, and his antipathy for women and people of color. Craziness is just our ethical Photoshop, smoothing out our blemishes and airbrushing away our love handles so that we may gasp and coo at our own illusory reflections.

It probably won't surprise you, Gyasi, that to my eyes there is no shortage of profoundly disheartening phenomena that are endemic to modern life—like the unrepentant destruction of the environment, economic policy that rewards those most willing to ruthlessly grasp and exploit, the negligible value of human life, and a chemical-saturated food supply of dubious healthfulness, to name but a few. We're caught in a proposition not unlike the conundrum of fighter pilot John Yossarian in Joseph Heller's *Catch-22*. Yossarian chafed at the contradiction that policy allowed only madmen to leave the army, while common sense told him that no sane person deliberately imperils himself in war. Likewise, American culture compels us to believe that suicide is an irrational desire to force one's way out of a demonstrably absurd world. Our conceptions of what it means to be mentally ill are often undergirded by this self-justifying imperative, a need to centralize willingness to accept and reproduce the status quo as the touchstone of sanity. Should one omit that criterion, as Bad Religion muses we should, it's not hard to imagine how depression could, in fact, be a healthy reaction to a sick civilization.

I say so not as an endorsement of nihilism, but out of recognition that being happy in a robustly unjust world is an achievement of meticulous self-regulation, of the fraught straining to excavate silver linings. Resisting despair is an act of faith and defiance more than it is a reasonable reaction to living a reality that consistently outpaces satire. You'd have to be crazy to be happy.

○ ○ ○ ○

My friendship with Chance Lyles was forged by a shared love of various countercultures, a thirst for extemporaneous adventure, and a mutual horror at the looming predictability and obligation of adulthood. So it's probably fitting that he subverted my expectations from the first day that we met. On move-in day of my sophomore year of college, Chance, who lived in the dorm across the hall from me, overheard me jumping on my bed and noodling aimlessly on my Gibson Les Paul at what I now realize was a woefully inconsiderate volume. When he knocked on my door, I opened it in a huff and affected my most cantankerous glare in preparation for him to tell me to turn it down. Instead, he told me to turn it up.

"I play too, dude," he drawled in his disarmingly unpretentious midwestern accent, gesturing at a tangled assortment of noisemaking paraphernalia he'd hauled into his own room across the hall that morning. He was a freckled, dreadlocked kid with the kind of perpetually drowsy eyes that suggested a fondness for the ganj. "Wanna jam, dog?"

We were both new transfer students at a small Quaker school. Although the college was known for its tolerant vibe and left-leaning politics, I was skeptical I'd be any less of an oddball there then I'd been everywhere else. But then I met Chance. We had been assigned to the same dorm because we'd both taken "gap years" (he'd been out of school for two while I'd been on an academic sabbatical for a whopping five), and found ourselves bemused by the unintentionally patronizing New Student Orientation activities appropriately conceived for eighteen-year-olds who were just a step or two removed from wetting the bed. Soon we were filling the week before the official start of classes with long, meandering blunt rides in his car, during which he'd light up and tell me stories about tripping on Robitussin in the snowy hills of Muncie, Indiana. I would stare out the window, listening intently, or man the iPod and set the mood using his impressively expansive and varied record collection, which ranged from the spastic math rock that was popular in my town to Japanese-language bands I'd never heard of, whose lyrics were completely opaque but instinctually perfect to me.

Some afternoons Chance and I would hike the dense woods in the back of campus and argue about the viability of the hulking brown mushrooms that grew everywhere: was eating them a slick evasion of the less-than-appetizing dining hall or a courtship of instant death? He'd recently read Jack Kerouac's *The Dharma Bums* and was taken with protagonist Japhy Ryder's intrepid, rough-and-tumble approach to self-reliance, while I, a dude with extensive food allergies, was more attracted to author surrogate Ray Smith's more cautious variety of Buddhist transcendence. We both appreciated the symbiosis of our relation to the respective characters. We bonded over our shared intention to pursue a bhikkhu life, what Ryder described as a vision of "thousands, or even millions of young Americans wandering around refusing to subscribe to the general demand that they consume production and therefore have to work for the privilege of consuming all that crap they didn't really want anyway, such as refrigerators, TV sets, cars, at least fancy new cars, certain hair oils and deodorants, etc."[3] I'd eventually learn Chance hadn't come to this conclusion lightly and that, in fact, his disaffection had been a source of considerable unease just a few years prior.

"It was a big deal for me to find *Dharma Bums* and Cap'n Jazz and shit," he'd tell me on a blunt ride, as jittery guitar lines writhed in stereo and rustic pastures whizzed by in the rearview mirror. "For the longest time I just thought I was *crazy*, dude."

Early in the school year, he'd wandered in to my room clutching the liner notes booklet from the seminal post-hardcore band Cap'n Jazz's vinyl double-LP *Analphabetapolothology*. "I feel like you'd get down to this," he said before chucking the booklet on my bed and disappearing across the hall. I inspected the liner notes to find a personal essay written by frontman Tim Kinsella about his lifelong battle with crippling anxiety. The short but powerful rumination on preserving hope and optimism in the face of life's vicissitudes was capped off with a memorable dictum: "the will to live is the will to pursue the will to live." It proved to be a timely recommendation of reading material. That night, I quoted Kinsella's manifesto and recommended the essay in its entirety in an email to a friend from home who was tussling with suicidal thoughts herself.

When I interview Chance for this book, it has been three years since we met in college and Chance is living in Japan. He is supporting himself by working as an English teacher. Though there are other recent graduates of the college's vaunted Japanese Studies program living in Japan's urban centers, Chance lives in the mountains in relative isolation. We are still in fairly regular correspondence, and his mention of reading *Catch-22* for the first time is actually the catalyst for this annotation and for the addition of "Pity the Dead" to your mixtape.

"One of the things about *Catch-22* is that that concept has been present in my mind since I was 18," he writes me one day. "Crazy people don't think they are crazy, and I've thought I was crazy since I was 18, so I must not be crazy."

○ ○ ○ ○

I was intrigued by the enlightening possibilities of perceived madness before I knew what punk was. In the midnineties, a popular Pizza Hut commercial featured NBA superstar David "the Admiral" Robinson convincing notorious bad boy and fellow hooper Dennis "the Worm" Rodman that the brand's new stuffed-crust pizza was best enjoyed when eaten backward.[4] Being a budding basketball enthusiast and die-hard lover of pizza, I was fascinated with the commercial as a youngster. My knowledge of the game allowed me to appreciate the contrast between Rodman's persona as the impish oddball on the otherwise all-business Chicago Bulls 1996–98 championship teams, and Robinson's aura as an upstanding do-gooder whose nickname alluded to his two years of navy service, starting in 1987 when he was drafted and ending in 1989 when he began his professional career. The ad featured Robinson insisting that Rodman eat the pizza's crust first, while Rodman expressed skepticism, saying "You crazy man, you crazy!" The humor came from the perception that the famously androgynous and heavily-tattooed Rodman was, in fact, the crazy one, and even he was discombobulated by the notion of flouting pizza-eating convention. Watching the commercial with our father when I was around eight years old, I thought I'd untangled the supposed irony.

"That's so funny," I said to my dad. "He thinks it's crazy to eat pizza backwards and he has no idea everyone else thinks *he* is crazy."

"No, he's very aware of that, actually," Baba said sharply, then an avid NBA observer himself. "Dennis Rodman certainly knows other people think he's crazy."

It didn't compute. If being crazy meant that one was detached from reality, how could someone accurately recognize that others perceived him as crazy and still be crazy? At first, I had assumed that Rodman's pesky antics on the court and flamboyant attire off it were the product of a slightly unsound mind. But the suggestion that Rodman understood exactly how others viewed him was an important new wrinkle to my still-brewing notion of sanity's limits. It was a critical distinction that Rodman's reputation was something he cultivated by choice. An inability to recognize the consensus reality and the decision to defy it are not one and the same, but the two are often conflated within the colloquialisms we use about crazy. If Rodman had actively decided to embrace his own views about gender, apparel, and even sportsmanship, it was reductive to dismiss him as a nutcase. Surely he was more like a revolutionary.

In the year to come, my intrigue with Dennis Rodman grew and culminated with my choosing to dress as the NBA's all-time rebounding champion for Halloween in fourth grade. The morning of Halloween, the Black Momba carefully applied a gaudy concoction of makeup to my cheeks and eyes and suffused my short, cropped Afro with electric green spray-in hair dye. I'd winced in discomfort as she fastened the clip-on nose ring I'd been thrilled to find at the dollar store the evening before, but I smiled to myself when I scanned the completed look in the bathroom mirror. By the time I arrived in class, my face had become accustomed to the thick layers of makeup and the clunky nose jewelry so that I'd all but forgotten I was in costume. It took me a few moments to interpret the significance of the pointed scowl the principal shot me as I strode into my homeroom.

"Happy Halloween, Mrs. Connors," I offered, thinking she'd soften. The icy stare proved resilient.

"Well, you need to keep that put away until then," she said, shuddering.

I did as I was instructed, but the novelty of my hair and face alone proved to be a lightning rod for both praise and criticism all that morning. I had expected the costume to shock and awe to some degree. Given that Halloween's general purpose was to dress in clothing and take on identities that were not permissible the other 364 days of the year, I couldn't imagine that mimicking the Worm's signature look for the day was any more appalling a choice than the more pedestrian ghosts, zombies, and vampires that surrounded me during the classroom holiday party. I started to get an inkling that maybe I'd overstepped the holiday's boundaries when two classmates I knew from the soccer team began staring at me and exchanging whispers that afternoon. I was unable to make out most of the conversation, but it seemed to center on "why G'Ra's parents would let him come to school looking like a crazy faggot."

In my nine-year-old naivete, I was shocked to hear this from fellow jocks. Dennis Rodman and his eccentricity were well known. Couldn't they see I was just playing at being the star power forward for fun? But the incident helped to reconcile for me the tension between Rodman's alleged craziness and his awareness of the world's low regard for him. He was threatening to the sporting establishment because he was an athletic dynamo of unquestionable physical and mental toughness, yet he was comfortable appearing in public in dresses and mascara. For those who remained committed to outmoded ideas about masculinity and "decency," it was easier to frame Rodman's look as lunacy than to recognize him as a gadfly.

Of course, I was too young to fully understand the sexual politics at work, but I could already appreciate that something about Dennis Rodman's exotic, gender-bending persona ran afoul of some hallowed code. After that day, I also knew my willingness to engage with that androgyny made me "crazy" too, in the eyes of my classmates. The implications of that association remained murky, but one thing was clear: there was more at stake in the public's general estimation of the Worm than the relative oddness of stuffed-crust pizza.

Reading *The Bell Jar* in college provided another case study. Throughout our discussion of the book, the male professor who taught the class repeatedly directed attention to "textual clues to the main character's instability," while insisting that he was approaching the novel without a particular agenda. Never mind that being a gifted, ambitious woman in a cultural milieu that insisted upon the repression and domestication of all women would cause anyone with angst. Admittedly, the fact that *The Bell Jar* is widely read as the loosely fictionalized autobiography of a writer who took her own life plays heavily into the interpretation that protagonist Esther Greenwood is driven chiefly by madness rather than principled dissent. Nonetheless, the emphasis on this component of the novel's context suggests a hesitance to mark the culpability of the social conventions that constrained her. It troubled me that a professor could land on mental illness as the central takeaway of a story about an imaginative, passionate person who bristled at having to reduce herself to fit a social role she didn't choose.

I saw Esther Greenwood as the kind of figure Jack Kerouac describes when he writes, "All our best men are laughed at in this nightmare land."[5] In view of the Beat ethos that grounded Kerouac's proclamation, the surest indication that Greenwood was on a trajectory that might lead to transcendence was the fact that her sexual, artistic, and intellectual inclinations so thoroughly unsettled those around her. Even in an academic context in which critical thinking was supposedly encouraged, the course's analysis of a canonical text ultimately served to legitimize the position that one who struggles against an establishment that persecutes her is suffering from an affliction. By contrast, while examining the patriarchal attitudes espoused by the male characters in *The Bell Jar,* the professor never missed an opportunity to remind us that such views were "typical of their time." (Somehow, no one identifies the 1960s as a time of widespread mental instability among men.) In effect, an objectively baseless perspective—like say, the belief that a human's worth is chiefly determined by whether or not she remains virginal until marriage—and a logical one—like Greenwood's objection to neglecting her literary gifts for the benefit of a domestic life—were made to change places. As our class discussion framed it, patriarchy was not a symptom of illness, but mere normalcy. Misnaming Esther Greenwood's woe at being tragically miscast in a gender-rigid play always seemed to me like the remix to drapetomania, an "illness" invented by pseudoscientist Samuel Cartwright in 1851 to explain African Americans' attempts to escape slavery. What better way to normalize a barbaric institution than to diagnose its antagonists as medically unwell? To our contemporary moral compasses, drapetomania is an egregious example of an empowered group framing insanity as whatever that is disadvantageous to their interests, but it is more representative of a pattern than our national mythology admits.

Asim family lore relied upon its own myths, one of which was rehearsed every quarter of my entire junior high school career. At Eastern Middle School, report cards were issued four times a year on the first of a month. I'd earned the elite grades and test scores to be admitted to the grueling program, but for a number of reasons—including but not limited to the onset of hormones and my discovery of punk rock—my performance went into a tailspin once I started taking classes. Abysmal student that I was, report card day made my life something like the inverse of that Bone Thugs song "1st of tha month," which praises the triumphant day in the projects when welfare checks come out. It wasn't just that my mother would lecture me for hours about how shiftless and disappointing a son I was. It was mostly how I could count on her busting out one of her greatest hits, a tearful monologue about a recurring dream she had that dramatized the upward mobility rhetoric she used to shame me for my indifference to academic success.

In the dream, a woman who resembles my mother is aboard what is presumably a sixteenth-century slave ship. Kidnapped Africans in shackles are leaping off the deck into shark-infested waters, going full Patrick Henry in choosing death over the surrender of their liberty to the slave profiteers steering the vessel. As the Black Momba tells it, her presumed forbear peers over the side of the ship and considers plunging in but instead halts before glancing pensively at her swollen belly. This is the part when my mother's vision (and incredibly convenient moral trump card) becomes too Hollywood to stomach. The pregnant African woman turns to look across time at our mother, and when the woman knows she's got our mother's attention, she winks and steps back from the edge of the ship.

"I recognize that wink," my mother would say breathlessly. "All the women on my mother's side of the family wink that way. She's letting me know that she endured the unimaginable for a purpose: so that I might live."

In a vacuum, I guess I might find that story moving, if not entirely persuasive. I sympathize, of course, with the impulse to find meaning in the residue of traumatic history. But this eerie analepsis was usually a device for the Black Momba to argue that my shoddy GPA was a disgrace to our nameless, faceless ancestors who'd survived the middle passage.

"If those who came before you could persevere in the face of torture, disease, malnutrition, and Jesus knows what else," my mother said often, "the least you can do is turn some damn homework in on time!"

The will to live is the will to pursue the will to live. Her moral hectoring lingered with me, even if it didn't ignite the scholastic spark the Black Momba hoped for. All through seventh grade, I'd imagine a cohort of emaciated brown bodies hovering around my desk and shaking their heads at me with quiet despondence every time I was handed back another test with a giant, crimson D marked across the top.

I get it. Survival at all costs is a practical mandate when your lineage is freighted with a history of subjugation and terror. Enduring that legacy and its echoes takes determination.

Recognizing what your predecessors have already overcome can help. Still, there was something about my mother's recurring dream and the accompanying rhetoric that seemed to enforce a kind of complacence, a willingness to bear the intolerable no matter what.

○ ○ ○ ○

I was more attracted to the Afrofuturist Drexciya myth, a tale of an underwater civilization populated by the unborn children of pregnant African women. In this fictionalization of real-world atrocity, their babies learned to breathe underwater while still in the womb. The would-be enslaved women descended into the ocean to find not death but an Atlantean civilization that welcomed them and their rapidly evolved progeny. I understand that we descended from the types of people whose will to live persisted over centuries of rape, starvation, violence, and bondage. I'm just not so sure that everyone who granted the calm, cool Atlantic's supplications for kisses was a coward.

Ever Since I Was
a Little Grrrl

An Annotation of Black Kids'
"I'm Not Gonna Teach Your Boyfriend
How to Dance with You"

"**A**fter the feminist revolution comes—and women everywhere have come together to overthrow male domination—you and Eric are the kind of men I might be willing to consider keeping as pets."

Ashanti told me this without taking her eyes off the road. She was maneuvering a rental car through downtown Philadelphia traffic, and we'd just dropped Eric off to meet up with his boyfriend. I've told Ashanti a few times that she resembles a real-life Disney princess both in terms of her personality and her appearance. She's tenacious in a way that made the ferocity of the comment unsurprising, and she's disarmingly pretty in a way that padded its landing. Ashanti, Eric, and I had been working closely together for the past two months at a black feminist social justice organization. That afternoon, we were returning to New York City after attending a work retreat in rural Pennsylvania. The group had been debriefing about the retreat, and the conversation had drifted toward how gender informs group dynamics in a professional context. Plenty of men drawn to the kind of work we did would announce themselves as feminists, Ashanti pointed out, but it could not be taken as a given that such men would actually be comfortable taking orders from women and collaborating with women as intellectual equals. It was Ashanti's view that Eric and I lived up to our billing as feminists—not just in terms of making meaningful contributions to woman-centered social justice projects, but in terms of how we conducted ourselves alongside our female colleagues.

Gyasi, I don't tell you this as some kind of humblebrag. It was not the first time that a progressive black woman had, backhandedly and with some surprise, christened me a user-friendly black man. I didn't rush home to add it to my CV or anything. Men's gender justice literacy is always graded on a curve. Brothers get inordinate props for being even slightly less patriarchal than the norm.

I mention Ashanti's observation in order to highlight the often negligible opportunity cost of male feminism. In our case particularly, Eric and I weren't exactly gender traitors. I'm not so sure that taking up residence in a post-revolution hamster cage would actually constitute a profound demotion from our respective statuses under patriarchy.

Eric was a bookish, black South African, a recent LLM graduate in his late twenties, and we'd made fast friends. He was warm and witty and seemed to instantly enchant nearly everyone with his casual eloquence and sonorous bass voice.

Days earlier Eric and I discussed how the shared qualities that made us compatible homies were probably the same ones that made us the female feminist's most intuitive allies. Though he had grown up in Malawi and South Africa, both of us had coming-of-age experiences in which it was constantly alleged that our interests and temperaments were somehow not manly and not black. On each of our respective continents, being intellectually curious, relatively gentle, introspective, and—interestingly—*knowledgeable about rock music* apparently defied the rubrics of manhood and blackness alike. Eric's sexuality eventually made his variance from the masculine ideal perhaps more readily legible, but his friends and acquaintances regarded him as an unusual man before he ever came out. Actual queerness is a sufficient but unnecessary condition for being branded "soft," that nebulous, damning repository for all things contrary to respectable manliness. Likewise, I was presumed to be gay so often during my teens and early twenties that I periodically wondered if everyone else knew something I didn't. The specter of homosexuality always attaches to a wider lot than its reality does.

For the compassionate, thinking man, embracing feminism isn't this magnanimous concession so much as it is canny self-preservation. If there were no women around, patriarchy would still have a pecking order in which intellectual, emotionally literate dudes would be somewhere near the bottom. In fact, patriarchy often constructs those qualities as feminine and thus undesirable. Being smart and sensitive while black and male—and mocked as girlish for being that way—can in a best-case scenario catalyze a dawning of feminist consciousness. Sooner or later you realize that having characteristics in common with women is not being stigmatized simply because you aren't one. The maligning of an entire gender buttresses a power structure that compromises your own freedom, too.

It's fitting that one of pop culture's most striking illustrations of this occurred on HBO's *The Wire*, a show that is famously unflinching in its depiction of all permutations of male brutishness. We meet sixteen-year-old Wallace as a fledgling drug dealer in a low-rise housing project in Baltimore. The events of the show take place not far from where Mom and Baba owned a house from 2006 to 2009, or where you briefly attended public elementary school. Wallace and his lifelong friends Bodie and Poot are foot soldiers of the Barksdale Organization, but there are cues that Wallace stands out from the local knuckleheads. One of the lieutenants in the organization says as much, encouraging Wallace to abandon the street life in order to reenroll in ninth grade to realize his scholastic potential, even though Wallace is by this time two years older than the typical freshman.

His aptitude quickly proves to be an asset to the organization. When the stash that he and his friends preside over is stolen, it's Wallace who spots the thief's accomplice playing pinball at a local hangout. Wallace informs his bosses, who arrange to have the accomplice captured and tortured to death. They leave the disfigured body in public view to send a message to the neighborhood, and Wallace is so disgusted by this outcome that he decides he wants no part of the drug trade anymore. Initially, the Barksdale Organization allows Wallace to quietly step aside, even sending him off with a kind of severance package in the form of a share of the bounty that had been placed on the slain man's head. But eventually, Wallace's former superiors in the drug cabal get wind of his cooperation with police. To stop the teenager before he can incriminate them further, Bodie and Poot's bosses issue an order to kill Wallace. In a heartbreaking scene that is among the show's most memorable, Bodie and Poot corner Wallace in a barren project bedroom and Bodie pulls a gun.

"Yo—y'all my niggas, yo," Wallace pleads.[1]

"You brought this on yourself," Bodie replies before gathering his nerve and shooting his erstwhile friend.

Bodie and Poot being Wallace's niggas crystallizes the tenuous and conditional nature of fraternity. The promise of masculine acceptance is contingent on adherence to a code of self-interested cruelty.

Tellingly, characters on *The Wire* are endlessly questioning or lauding each other's "heart," but in the chest-thumping vernacular of the street, the strength of that muscle determines how bold one is in combat, not one's willingness to feel. Remorse, empathy, and tenderness are scorned openly and punished forcefully. Throughout the first season, Wallace was the character on *The Wire* I most identified with. The implications of this affinity were familiar and unsettling. Black patriarchy doesn't have a place for someone like Wallace. It is threatened by someone like him and will readily dispose of him despite the fact that his racial, gender, and class identity should mean he's a natural fit for the boys' club.

If this is the predicament of the black man who feels, and thinks no less of himself for doing so, patriarchy offers few compelling incentives for people like you and me to uphold it. Maybe I'm tripping, but picking between Ashanti's leash and Bodie's gun doesn't seem to be any kind of Sophie's Choice.

For better or worse, the traits that would make me inevitably subject to that crossroads were manifest at an early age. You've probably heard the story in which I purported to "test Newton's laws" at a neighborhood gym by pressing my weight into one of the walls and loudly asking why, if every action has an equal and opposite reaction, the walls didn't seem to be pushing me back. (Of course, the walls were, but I was eight years old, so I imagined Newton meant that a pair of rippling biceps would emerge from the architecture and knock me on my backside.) Another black boy about my age saw my makeshift physics experiment and misinterpreted it as a show of force. He began pressing on the same wall, baring his teeth at me and grunting as if to say *oh, two can play that game.*

You could say Mom and Baba sought to rescue me from a fate like Wallace's. First by enrolling me in an expensive private school on the other side of town, and eventually by fleeing urban St. Louis altogether in favor of the relatively affluent neighborhood we lived in before moving again to Baltimore. I was nine and Joe was thirteen when Baba received job offers from the *Chicago Tribune*, the *New York Times*, and the *Washington Post* all at once. The convergence of these opportunities struck Mom as providential, because at the time Joe and I both occupied the demographic sweet spot for recruitment as Crips. Every day that the Asim Team remained on our block presented a chance for the scourge of gang violence to ensnare Joe and me deliberately and directly, as opposed to merely making us collateral damage. Dating back to my earliest memories of urban St. Louis, the threat of that violence lurked in my peripheral vision, and I had a vague foreboding that becoming a teenager would usher me into the direct line of fire.

I had a few close encounters with the Crip kind, but none more impactful than the time Mom tried to teach me to ride a bike. Joe had learned to ride a few years earlier, and I was still getting used to a tricycle. Mom offered to take us to the park up the street, as it was a rare source of forgiving terrain fit for learning to balance on a two-wheeler.

I had looked forward to the trip for days. All of the girls and boys in the neighborhood that Joe and I played with could already ride. Even Warren, a chubby momma's boy with asthma who was the target of just about everyone's derision, could pop some pitiful approximation of a wheelie. I was determined to shore up what felt like a conspicuous weakness. Fairground Park was only a few blocks from our house, but it was farther than Joe and I were allowed to travel on our own. Even on my short jaunts up and down the crumbling sidewalks outside our home, I'd noticed that the concrete grew smoother beneath my tricycle tires whenever I rode far enough that the Fairgrounds Park entrance was in sight. Infrastructure that was intact was so unusual in our part of North St. Louis that you noticed even the subtle gradations of upkeep. I figured that if someone saw the pavement en route to the park as worthy of maintenance, then maybe being in the park was closer to being someplace people actually cared about. With Mom in tow, we were finally allowed to venture into a sector of the neighborhood that felt novel and exciting.

That day, before Joe, Mom, and I even entered the park, a gunfight broke out between two sets of gangbangers situated kitty-corner to one another. One group of gun-toting youths were firing from the park's entrance, while their rivals blasted back from an alley thirty yards away. Mom, Joe, and I had the misfortune of having walked in between them.

I'd heard gunshots ring out in our neighborhood so often that it did not immediately register as an indication of mortal peril. "Stay away from the windows" was a signal refrain of our childhood bedtime rituals. The nightly danger of stray bullets was as routine as the appearance of lightning bugs. I only began to appreciate the gravity of the situation when the Black Momba froze. She angled her body between us and the two sets of gunmen and motioned for Joe and me to halt behind her.

One of the bangers who'd been shooting glanced over his shoulder to fire across the alley once more, then took off running into Fairground Park. If we trekked onward to our destination as planned, we'd be effectively tailing at least one of the gunmen. We also had no way of knowing whether the skirmish we'd inadvertently become caught in was a subset of a larger melee or if reinforcements for either of the two warring crews lurked deeper in the park. A serene afternoon turned ghastly in an instant.

"Ride home, Joe," Mom instructed. "Go quickly."

Joe didn't need to be told twice. He shifted his weight on his handsome, green-and-white ten-speed, pushed off with his right foot and pedaled like his life depended on it. The Black Momba had separate instructions for her bike-inept son.

"G'Ra, run. Leave the bike and run. Follow your brother."

I let go of the bike and then hesitated, because the Black Momba didn't seem to be running. I stared dumbly as she gathered up the two-wheeler handed down to me when Joe got an even cooler bike for his tenth birthday. She reversed course and began walking back toward our house at a casual pace. As bullets whizzed less than thirty yards away, I found myself rapidly analyzing the stakes. We were poor enough that if she did leave the bike behind, it was not likely we could afford to replace it anytime soon. But it was clear to me that the situation might claim at least one of two potential casualties—the bike I'd yet to learn to ride or Mom—and she seemed to be prioritizing the less important one. Even if she wanted to bring the bike with us, why did *she* have to carry it?

I was famously underweight at the time, anemic even. Baba spoon-fed me liquid iron every morning at the behest of our pediatrician. Yet fear made me believe I could chuck that bike on my slight shoulders and schlep it to safety if it meant expediting Mom's own escape. Mothers are funny. Ours wouldn't hesitate to shout at the top of her lungs over my always-overdue library books, but in the heat of a life-threatening predicament, she remained eerily calm.

"Go on, G'Ra," she urged again. "Run on."

I could see Joe speeding away in the distance. I glanced uneasily at Mom once more and finally took off. My enduring memory of sprinting home from Fairgrounds Park was the powerlessness I felt, the gnawing certainty that my inability to ride a bike was going to get my mother killed. With each frantic step, I was bracing myself for the sound of a killing shot, not to my own tiny body but to Mom's. Naturally I was not consciously thinking about gender very often yet, but I knew boys were meant to be strong, heroic, and in control. As you know, Joe and Baba were and are major comic book heads. Joe's expansive oeuvre of drawings of superheroes adorned our shabby walls. They were images of masculine virility and power that I'd failed to mirror when the real-life counterparts of supervillains had endangered my own mother.

We all made it home unscathed at our various paces. I wouldn't learn to balance on two wheels until our move to the suburbs years later. The Black Momba eventually explained that her actual decision-making in that harrowing moment had nothing to do with being impeded by my bike. She figured onlookers might interpret the sight of Joe pedaling furiously and me hauling narrow six-year-old butt behind him as children merely behaving as children do. If Mom had taken off at top speed behind us, the police or potentially even other bangers might conclude she was involved with the crossfire we'd narrowly escaped.

Not being able to ride a bike, stop bullets, or protect my mother and feeling deep shame about all of the above was this early realization that my ability to meet the imperatives of maleness is constrained by race and class. I understood that the terror unleashed by gangs was endemic to the "bad neighborhood" we lived in, and I knew that living there had something to do with being black. The awareness that there might be some amount of daylight between me and the masculine ideal, and that this gap was at least partially attributable to the ways that money and color circumscribed my life, seems disconcertingly in league with the thesis that Daniel Patrick Moynihan advanced about black disaffection in 1965. If black feminism wasn't available as a corrective, I might believe I was saddled with the affliction that Moynihan claimed was affecting African American men writ large.

In an influential report titled *The Negro Family: The Case for National Action*, Moynihan concludes that the emasculation of black men is the primary obstacle to the entire race's progress. In Moynihan's eyes, black America was matriarchal because women were the primary breadwinners in a disproportionate number of black households and because black women outperformed their male counterparts in educational attainment and professional prestige. Moynihan's findings have remained a popular framework for understanding the condition of African American life in the half century since the report's publication. Hoteps don't often mention Moynihan by name, but his ideas are articles of faith among ankh necklace enthusiasts. As you can imagine, only a masculinist reading would determine that racism's most pernicious consequence is the asymmetry between the dominance society confers on white men and the supposed abjection it confers on black men. This misguided thinking has led many black men not only to respond to the perceived prosperity of our sisters as a threat but to view white male dominance as something worth aspiring to.

The specious appeal of that outlook is no mystery to me. Especially when I remember how it felt to flee Fairgrounds Park with the smell of gun smoke in the air and Mom lagging defenseless behind me. But being the square peg to conventional masculinity's round hole is less burden than blessing. It's an opportunity to refashion the self using something other than the oppressor's likeness as a prototype. The logic of reclaiming a term or idea traditionally used to derogate and exclude usually escapes me. I think it's possible, though, that Moynihan correctly identified a fulcrum in African American life; only he used it to pivot in the wrong direction. As a black male punk rocker, gender disrepair feels to me like an aperture of radical possibility. What would it mean to shift from lamenting that racism keeps us from enjoying the full privileges of maleness to recognizing those diminished returns as incentive to divest from patriarchy altogether? Why couldn't gender disrepair be reason to enhance our empathy rather than protect our privilege?

In fairness to those hanging on to patriarchy for dear life, I've had a bit of a head start on this tip. For the inaugural week of sixth grade, I was a girl. The elementary school I had attended the prior spring did not feed into my new middle school, so I was entering a social environment where I knew almost no one. That summer I had grown my hair long enough to braid. I was eleven years old and, physically speaking, something of a late bloomer—puberty had left no perceptible fingerprints as of yet. I didn't see myself as a feminine kid, but between my relatively long eyelashes, corn-rowed hairstyle, and my "exotic" and potentially unisex name, kids and adults at my new school more readily received me as a girl. I could understand how my gender might not have been immediately obvious, but I was shocked to realize that there had been such an easy consensus that I was not a guy. The moment of clarity came in gym class when a lively McGwire versus Sosa debate on the bleachers with a fellow male baseball fan came to a screeching halt. As I stood up mid-sentence and prepared to line up to receive a gym locker assignment, he cautioned me about following him into the boys' locker room.

"The girls' locker room is over that way," he'd said with an unnerving matter-of-factness.

All at once, the strangeness I'd felt all week but couldn't put my finger on came into sharp focus. The clique of female gel pen aficionados who'd provisionally accepted me into their group by inviting me to sit with them at lunch had done so under a false impression. The boy who sat next to me in home room—the one who had stared at me all week with an intensity I found utterly alien—was similarly misinformed. I had been selected considerably later than I was accustomed to in the pick-up basketball games sixth graders played every weekday morning before the bell rang. Each of these experiences began to make sense upon being directed to the girls' locker room. Later in the school year when I recounted aloud the strange, reversible metamorphosis I'd undergone in September, a classmate confessed that she was "so disappointed" to find out I was a dude. She thought she'd "finally met another girl with a voice as deep as" hers.

My temporary reclassification showed precisely how fluid my belonging to any group was. If all I had to do to become a girl was grow my hair out and transfer schools, boyhood as an identity couldn't possibly be the sturdiest mooring. The realization of what Moynihan claims should have been my worst fear and deepest neurosis had come to pass, and my world didn't exactly come crashing down. I didn't aspire *not* to be a boy, but I didn't feel particularly territorial about it, either. Having a formative experience of passing as a girl contributed to my attraction to alternative culture, and, on some level, I'm certain it informed my budding politics. Emasculation had happened—and nothing happened. How freeing! I was relieved of the compulsion to overcompensate for the withholding of patriarchal power many black men believe would be theirs if not for race.

Gravitating to punk was safer once this happened. Yes, liking any kind of music other than rap was "soft." But how bad could it be to be soft, if without trying I'd been unceremoniously transfigured into a straight-up girl? I wasn't actively looking to become more feminine so much as limit the degree to which I'd be subject to compulsory masculinity, and there were aspects of punk culture that offered more appealing models for manhood. At that age, speedy tempos, bright guitar riffs, and exuberant melodies also called to me in ways that had nothing to do with politics. There's probably something about the particular collision of pimples and puberty that endears the ears to music that sounds how a carbonated soft drink feels. But I also associated the sonic textures of punk music with freedom. I wanted to be around people and in proximity with music and art that encouraged pliability and elasticity in how masculinity was performed and understood.

Of course, that essentially meant searching for a reflection of the goings on at Asim HQ. My observation of our own parents has consistently revealed them to be devoted, fungible teammates in the most practical sense of the word. By the time you came along in the early 2000s, Mom and Baba had settled into a gender normative division of labor in which Mom ran the household and Baba earned the income. But before Baba's literary career took off, our parents ran the family like a strategic framework popularized by the Dutch national soccer team called "total football." Total football is a fluid team concept in which players are free to rotate between attacking, midfield, and defensive roles at will depending on what the on-field situation demands. When one player takes on a new role, the structure of the team remains intact because another player steps into the position that was just vacated. In most of my earliest memories, Mom was the primary breadwinner and Baba stayed home to write and manage the household.

Baba's conception of his own masculinity was expansive and resilient enough to accommodate the cheerful performance of the domestic tasks he undertook while Mom was out earning a paycheck. He cooked and cleaned, changed diapers, and completed the grocery shopping without incident or complaint. The Moynihan Report and its considerable ideological residue would have us believe that depriving Baba of the satisfaction that comes with being the family's main earner should be existentially unsettling for him, a source of consternation so profound that it inhibits his ability to function as a productive member of society.

By the same token, Moynihanism would hold that Mom was liable to become so disgusted by Baba's nonchalant embrace of traditionally feminine household duties that she'd lose respect for him. None of this came to pass. If black uplift truly relied on "men being men" and "women being women," you'd likely not have been born. The reason for the eight-year age gap between our sister, Indigo, and me is that after I was born, the Black Momba established some terms and conditions for the existence of further Asims. There could be no more children, she told Baba, until the family had hit particular benchmarks related to income and lifestyle. Mom had had me in a clinic and was fed up; it was the last pregnancy she would endure without an upgrade in care. It took several years of both of our parents working outside of the home before Mom's criteria were met, at which point she and Baba agreed that Mom would transition into a home-making role. Soon after she was pregnant with Indigo, Jelani and eventually you came along. What Moynihan frames as a deficiency proved to be anything but. Our mother's strength, competence, and vision didn't compromise our father's. Each magnified the other.

In fact, I'd wager that a total football marriage was a condition of possibility for our family's escape from poverty. Mom and Baba's fluid cooperation established a template for my own sense of gender roles—which is to say that for the most part I was inclined to see them as infinitely malleable. Only when I ventured outside of the household did I fully appreciate that particular work, temperaments, and communication styles were widely understood to correspond with one gender or the other.

The strength of patriarchy's hold on black men is as much about sexuality as it is about gender and race, especially for straight men. Most people's sense of heterosexuality is predicated on some notion of gender polarity. Men and women are opposites who can complement one another when united, rather than like entities that sometimes overlap. The sizzle that animates the pursuit of sexual fulfillment is sustained by interpersonal discord rather than harmony. Comity between genders short-circuits the snap, crackle, and pop of heterosexual electricity. The dramatic structure of romantic comedy even relies on the idea that men and women are so fundamentally different that they struggle to understand one another, and the challenge of spanning the distance between Mars and Venus is what makes the heartwarming denouement feel earned. To be a man who both desires and shares characteristics with women spoils the recipe for straight romantic love.

Depending on how you look at it, Black Kids' "I'm Not Gonna Teach Your Boyfriend How to Dance with You" either vindicates or undermines that recipe. The campy but infectious lead single from 2008's *Partie Traumatic* undulates with a distinctly Obama-era levity. Synthesized strings swell without self-consciousness, fearing neither schmaltz nor softness. Pert background vocals chirp with the giddy precision of a high school cheerleading squad. I knew I was going to love the song based on the title and band name alone, before I ever heard a note of it. The band's name pokes fun at the often totalizing nature of race as a modifier of identity. *The kids involved here are black,* their handle announces to the world, *which is all you need to know about them.*

"I'm Not Gonna Teach Your Boyfriend How to Dance with You" was released in an era when people used the word "metrosexual" to describe straight men who took regular showers. That this mild variation from the norm needed to be marked with a new term reveals the depth of American investment in the belief that when it comes to gender roles, to be heterosexual is not to be heterodox.

Black Kids had other ideas. Who better to report from the frontlines on love in the time of gender disrepair? The subversion turns on male vocalist-guitarist Reggie Youngblood's repetition of the line "you are the girl that I've been dreaming of ever since I was a little girl." "Dance with You" is a bop worthy of your mixtape because it's the rare pop music expression of desire based on affinity rather than polarity. The dance between the speaker and his dream girl is seamless. Yet a competitor less adroit with the steps is firmly entrenched as boyfriend. A snappy chorus kiboshes the prospect of a *Queer Eye for the Straight Guy*–like quid pro quo between the song's speaker and the titular boyfriend. This romantic helter-skelter is never resolved: the rhythmically challenged boyfriend remains untutored, the dream girl unattained, the speaker unbowed.

What I mean to say to you, Gyasi, is that if gender disrepair is an aperture of radical possibility, then making good on those possibilities may begin with the breezy admission of having ever been a little girl. And it may demand always remaining at least a tiny bit girl. I want to make the case that being a product of gender disrepair can mean experiencing one's humanity in terms of surplus rather than one's manhood in terms of deficit. The escape hatch out of niggerdom may be found via leaning into our asymmetry with white patriarchy rather than straining to "correct" it.

In the contemporary movement for black lives, a quote taken from James Baldwin's appearance on *The Dick Cavett Show* in 1968 has gained broad traction. You've probably heard it, or seen references to it on the popular T-shirts emblazoned with the defiant slogan "I am not your Negro."

> What white people have to do is try to find out in their hearts why it was necessary for them to have a nigger in the first place. Because I am not a nigger, I'm a man.[2]

In Baldwin's formulation, to reject niggerdom is to assert an identity that is itself bound up in yet other oppressive hierarchies. (He doesn't say, "I'm not a nigger, I'm a *human*.") I want to envision an exodus from niggerdom that does not in turn ensure the exploitation and subordination of non-men. Though it's fashionable to propose that we do away with gender entirely, I offer post-sexism as a target in order to draw a parallel with Ishmael Reed's suggestion that America would be better off pursuing a post-racist society than merely a post-racial one. Imagine if black men en masse followed the lead of the black feminist lesbian organization Combahee River Collective, which rejected a zero-sum approach to gender-race politics. This selection from their statement, more so than Baldwin's immortal adage, is a North Star that might guide us to a future that is simultaneously post-sexist, post-homophobic, and post-racist:

> We believe that the most profound and potentially most radical politics come directly out of our own identity, as opposed to working to end somebody else's oppression. In the case of Black women this is a particularly repugnant,

dangerous, threatening and therefore revolutionary concept because it is obvious from looking at all the political movements that have preceded us that anyone is more worthy of liberation than ourselves. We reject pedestals, queenhood, and walking ten paces behind. To be recognized as levelly human is enough.[3]

I realize that a boy singing about a girl in terms that foreground his own girlness could strike some as appropriative. But what I hear in Youngblood's yearning is the faintest outline of a politics of difference without otherness. I like to imagine that the speaker and his dream girl's dance floor synergy is a form of love grounded by the recognition of level humanity rather than love that enlarges the self by miniaturizing another.

It could seem fanciful to talk of involvement with punk rock as any kind of salve to toxic masculinity when punk culture is on the whole as much of an outlet for fratty boorishness as it is an incubator for the opposite. For every sensitive, introspective, Propagandhi song, there are ten canonical tunes detailing a male protagonist's violent revenge fantasies about a treacherous lover. Where punk culture can appear, at a superficial level, to boast an emancipatory insouciance toward gender norms, it can at the same time rehearse regressive cultural scripts without batting a heavily mascaraed eyelash. Being less beholden to traditional male gender expression doesn't automatically translate to being less patriarchal.

Former Blink-182 guitarist Tom Delonge's polish-tipped fingers have strummed countless odes to sex with the listener's mother. Mid-aughts emo luminary Senses Fail sported a Buddhism-inspired band name and howled lyrics that interpolated Bukowski poems to distinguish their catalogue from the gaggle of desultory dirges adorning MySpace pages during the band's heyday. Their literary and dharmic bona fides didn't preclude them from using the same objectifying language and misogynistic imagery as their less enlightened counterparts.

The subculture's permissive approaches to male vulnerability, androgyny, and sentimentality allow men to eschew traditional pigeonholes, but it's almost like that mainly translates to giving dudes additional resources to bedevil women with. The obvious test of any oppositional subculture rests on the question of who benefits from an alternative set of values and whether the values are really in opposition with the dominant culture if they ultimately serve to expand and consolidate the power of its most advantaged participants.

When June Jordan writes, "A democratic state is not proven by the welfare of the strong but by the welfare of the weak," she could just as well be talking about Warped Tour.

One can easily fall into the habit of describing punk as if its social and political POV is exclusively male. To do so is to ignore the significant and tuneful interventions nonmen have been making in the subculture nearly since its inception to disrupt precisely this mischaracterization. Not only do I sympathize with the righteous truculence of new school feminist pop punkers like Bad Cop/Bad Cop, for instance, I *identify* with it. In their slam dance–worthy screeds against gender essentialism, male abusers, and casual misogyny, I recognize the same right to be hostile that I claim and mobilize in my own lifelong antiracist struggle, even if I am at times the deserving object of antisexist hostility. The symmetry between a female punk's embrace of stylized irreverence as a means of subverting sexist standards and my own gravitation to it as a tool of antiracist disalienation, doesn't exculpate me from antisexist indictment; it inculpates me. I should be doubly inclined to support the struggle of my nonmen sibling punks, and when I fail to do so, I'm effectively two times the turncoat.

For me, the pursuit of tenable gender politics and a comfortable (if not always legible) gender performance has been a hunt for a Goldilocksian mean. Traditional masculinity and its attendant politics was a nonstarter, maybe not even something I've ever had access to. It was the porridge too hot. Punk culture had its charms, but in most cases and most ways whiteness and patriarchy still reigned unchallenged. That was the porridge too cold. It's taken the synthesis of punk and black feminism to arrive at something just right, to approach being the person I've been dreaming of ever since I was a little girl.

Intersectionality, the black feminist touchstone coined and theorized by Kimberlé Crenshaw, has been central to that synthesis. The mention of intersectionality often engenders reflexive discomfort in black men, probably because we instinctively recognize it as a lens that threatens to minimize our concerns and perspectives within the already limited discursive terrain allocated to blackness. Intersectionality invites us to ask a set of questions intended to highlight where power and disadvantage flows and along which channels. From that perspective, it's hard to imagine a mode of inquiry more conducive to parsing the situation of black manhood.

One of the paradigms at which Crenshaw's writing often takes aim is the black male endangerment frame, a vision of African American society in which the welfare of black men and boys is positioned as the key indicator of our well-being as a people—usually at the direct expense of any consideration of the experiences of black women and girls. Moynihan plays no small role in this frame's popularity. It's presumed that black dudes are in the main "worse off" than our sisters, mothers, and significant others, and that because of our greater susceptibility to antiblack racism, our concerns should be the cornerstone of antiracist agendas.

Crenshaw's ongoing critique of antiracist politics applies in equal measure to the lion's share of punk scenes. She argues that a trickle-down approach to liberation—in which the most privileged members of a subordinate group are positioned as the bellwethers of the group's progress—rarely reaches and never properly serves a group's most vulnerable members. Being both a black man and a punk rocker is a position that has offered a front row seat for witnessing how ineffectual change making can be without an intersectional lens. It's incumbent upon us as black men to not only navigate our own endangerment but to refute attempts to mobilize our precarity as excuses to neglect or exclude black people who aren't men.

Which is part of why I say punk is the theory and black feminism is the practice. My experience in punk rock has lent credence to the urgency of mapping social injustice from a black woman's vantage point and looking at black women's intellectual tradition as a model for that process. The democratic values that punk stands for are hollow unless they're equitably distributed to people across all genders. Black feminism is the rubric for optimizing the reach of punk's emancipatory project.

To see myself as a punk rocker, I had to look past the fact that the genre's most visible avatars were white men. I knew that in many respects my experience didn't parallel those of Billie Joe Armstrong or Sid Vicious or Joe Strummer. But I recognized that a punk ethos was resonant with my interior life, regardless of whether that was easily reconciled with how the world saw me. Punk gave me significant reps in the same exercise I would need to embrace black feminism. In the same way whiteness doesn't dissuade me from being punk, maleness doesn't dissuade me from being feminist.

○ ○ ○ ○

In Rudyard Kipling's "If—," the great reward for maintaining the laudable moral equilibrium he spends the first several stanzas delineating is to "be a Man, my son." It would be a wonderfully affirming poem, but the conditional statement upon which it's predicated leads us to a mistaken conclusion. There's no causal relationship between being discerning, generous, and resilient and being a man. As older brother writing to younger brother, I may be tempted to traffic in that same pattern of masculine advice transmission, where "manhood" is the promised land and my writing is Google Maps. Which means that here I have an opportunity to be a real punk, to substantively thumb my nose at tradition by turning conventional wisdom on its head. I hope to be the person who touts Combahee rather than Baldwin as the metric for your growth. What kind of equity is made possible when people aspiring to be their ideal selves set their sights on being human, rather than on being men? I implore you to find out. I'd rather see you become a person no more or less exalted than other levelly human persons. A person who evaluates their own grandness based on how contagious they can make their own freedom.

To the Edge and Back

An Annotation of Brand New's
"Sic Transit Gloria . . . Glory Fades"

You know what I miss, Gyasi? Playdates. The Black Momba calling the mother of one of my friends and agreeing on a time and place when their children would link up to watch cartoons. There was a point when playing was actually so pivotal to my prepubescent agenda that our mother would schedule it for me. It warranted being planned. It was a priority over something.

It's the spring before I decide to finally attend four-year college, and you could say that nostalgia leads me to maintain a different sort of playdate with a different sort of friend. I am a freelance writer and musician, living in a spare room in a good friend's childhood home. In a few months I'll become a twenty-four-year-old sophomore transfer student at a college in the Midwest. In the meantime, I'm stretched out on a creaky twin bed in a filthy bedroom in College Park,

Maryland, awaiting the return of Taisha: poet, activist, consummate make-out partner, and owner of the most beguiling sneer I've yet laid eyes on. I can't quite say that we have a schedule, and I suspect we rendezvous a bit more often than I ever got invited to play as a maladroit fourth-grader, but I relish these get-togethers with a similar zeal. Then again, the comparison probably doesn't hold up after that, because our late-night trysts beat the hell out of even the most idyllic boyhood afternoons of Legos and kickball.

"Don't you think you've gotten pretty enough in there? If you come back any hotter, you might make me insecure," I call to Taisha, trying to help my voice carry into the bathroom across the hall she has disappeared into for a proverbial "freshening up" session. I never know what to say to girls in these intimate situations, so I figure flattery can never be totally off target, especially to someone as unabashedly narcissistic as she is.

"There you go again, sweet talker," Taisha shouts back. "I'll be out in a minute. It's just that when the lights are on, I don't think you should have to see me with JBF hair."

I run the initials of all the US presidents I know through my head, and it's not working out for me.

"Oh, come on," she prods. "Not even you can be that green. You know."

"No, I don't."

"Just Been F—"

"Ah. Say no more."

There is a silence, and then the conversation I can never seem to avoid is imminent. I mentally count off the seconds until she launches into it. *3 . . . 2 . . . 1 . . .*

"Well, I guess I can't really have JBF hair with you, now can I? But you know, Just Been to Second Base Hair doesn't really have too great a ring to it." I can hear her sucking her teeth all the way from the bathroom, can easily picture her pouting into the mirror. I am calculating what kind of parry will be the quickest way *back* to second base.

"OK, but what about something clever like JB2B? I mean, it's supposed to be a sexual shorthand anyway, right?" The night's activities must've taken more out of me than I thought, because this is the best I've got.

"That sounds like the name of Luke Skywalker's third android sidekick. Like the sidekick to his sidekicks." Taisha emerges from the bathroom, saunters purposefully up to the twin bed in just her bra and panties.

"What's so wrong with just plain ol' JBF?" she purrs.

Perhaps I should explain why I am alone with a gorgeous woman and fretting about how to convince her *not* to have sex with me. For starters, by a loose definition, I'm a virgin. Now, lest you get carried away with visions of the kind of folly that made Steve Carell a household name, I should point out that I'm not a virgin merely incidentally, nor by virtue of romantic ineptitude. Since the ninth grade, I've rocked with the punk subculture called straight edge, which can be summed up pretty crudely as being anti-stupidity and operationalized as such: no drinking, no smoking, and no promiscuous sex. Punks and other like-minded outcast types tend to interpret the precepts of straight edge quite loosely. There is great variation in how and why edge becomes a part of people's lives, but it's essentially a tradition of socially conscious asceticism. There is no formal initiation process, but I'd adopted the core ideology early in high school and stuck with it despite encountering situations like these.

I don't know that sleeping with Taisha right now could really be called "promiscuous" sex. We clearly aren't a couple, but it's not as if I'm dating anyone else. On the other hand, when we were on the phone last week, Taisha told me how badly she wanted to eat her straight roommate out. And how disappointed she was that the roommate wasn't rolling. So far. What, pray tell, is the straight edge thing to do here?

The cost of my hesitation becomes clear when Taisha exhales sharply as a deflated party balloon. Suddenly steely, she makes a noise of irritation that defies onomatopoeia. The length of the interval between now and her admittedly tempting suggestion has offended her, and why shouldn't it? Like many women, she is not well-versed in the sexual politics of acting as the aggressor, and the novelty of the position annoys her.

"This is bullshit," she sighs as she dresses with alarming speed. "What the fuck is wrong with you?"

And not for the first time, I find myself frozen in disbelief in the batter's box, gaping stupidly at the inside corner of home plate, pondering the perhaps rash decision not to swing. Having struck out on a called third strike, my night is over.

It is said that the creative process is sparked from the realization that reality is incomplete. The observable world needs accoutrements, embroidery, a dash of panache, and the creative person goes about trying to deliver them. A similar deductive process led me to straight edge. Life underwhelmed me and I thought addition by subtraction could help me to feel a warm, comforting median of whelmed. I was a weekend warrior house flipper trying to turn an eyesore into an asset. At fourteen, I looked at the edifice of turn-of-the-century adolescence and mused, *hmm, this isn't doing it for me but maybe if we knocked out a few of these walls.*

Those walls were drugs, drinking, and promiscuous sex. I imagined that I wasn't doing so in a vacuum, but as a participant in straight edge.

I mentioned before that the first punk band I ever heard was Minor Threat, an iconic DC-based outfit that helped to popularize the subgenre called hardcore punk. Hardcore is punk on austerity measures. What it lacks in melody it makes up for in sheer fury, delivered by hoarse-throated vocals, brawny guitar tones, and thunderous drums. The straight edge movement is named after a song from Minor Threat's first EP, in which frontman Ian MacKaye rails against society's reliance on substances as a coping mechanism. MacKaye has largely downplayed the notion that the song was intended as a blueprint for a philosophy, but several generations of punk kids took it and ran with it. It has since become a voluntary lifestyle label for alienated punks who prefer their rebellion without a side of self-destruction. Though straight edge is chiefly associated with punk and hardcore, the scene's influence is expansive and has informed social justice movements and other music genres including metal, hip-hop, and folk.

It might seem counterintuitive that a punk rock movement would attempt and to some extent succeed at making asceticism cool. But I've always thought of straight edge as hardcore's minimalism taken to its logical conclusion: music marked by no-frills, unsentimental arrangements is a fitting soundtrack to a life devoid of substances and conquest-minded hookups. Straight edge kids have traditionally marked their hands and clothing with the letter x. The symbol is adapted from when doormen at clubs and bars would mark the hands of underage patrons with x's to indicate that they weren't allowed to buy alcohol. Though punk is more often noted for its nihilism than humanitarianism, the scene's revolutionary possibilities are central to its appeal for left-leaning, activist types. I was moved by the rhetoric that named straight edge as an approach to preserving the self and that self-destruction was counterproductive to the notion of investing in a more prosperous, peaceful collective future.

I suppose it's obvious to you that there were practical reasons to get with the program as well. You executed one of your best gags when you were eleven, by typing "How to Destroy G'Ra Asim" into a search engine and leaving the results screen up on my desktop while I was out for a run. Reading it when I returned, shining with sweat and flush with endorphins, was funny, but it also made the hairs on the back of my neck stand up. The sight of those pointedly capitalized words in the search bar created the sensation of having just missed a run-in with a superpowered archnemesis. One who'd infiltrated my room on a reconnaissance mission to find out how to vanquish me once and for all. Taking inventory of the real-life threats to my existence and realizing that they were legion was part of the self-evaluation process that led me to claim edge. That's probably because that superpowered archnemesis is, at least in a sense, real. A transhistorical adversary you can't call the police on because the police are in its employ. Straight edge had been up to that point a feeble, fallible counter to what the search engine would've conjured up, if it had interpreted the query the way you meant it.

I don't know the extent of your experience with substances or sex, but you've definitely got the disposition to be straight edge. The Black Momba complains that you're "difficult." The kinship I feel with you is based in part on this difficulty—a natural recalcitrance that is the seed of punk sensibility. Damian Genuardi, who played bass in the Explosion, calls it "looking at the world with a sort of skeptical eye, knowing things aren't right and trying to always be aware of that fact. It's having a certain dissatisfaction and being proud of having that dissatisfaction."[1] I'm not the kind of personality that becomes immediately impatient in moderate-length queues, files formal complaints about the service at restaurants, or corrects everybody's grammar at staff meetings. But I am the type that bristles at the easy ideological grooves social pressure coaxes us into. Which is to say, I'm a punk. I don't want to fall into any line unless I like where that line is going.

You have a similar distaste for conformism and a not wholly unrelated tactic for responding to it. When Indigo asks you about whether your friends push drugs and alcohol on you, you point out that your self-imposed isolation is a buffer: "I can't be subject to peer pressure if I don't have peers."

There's something to it. In your first year of public school in Baltimore in 2005, you were assigned a separate table during lunch time because the Black Momba had warned the school about your peanut allergy. To protect you from even the faintest possibility that a classmate's lunch might infect you, the lunch monitor made sure you sat alone. I worked as a classroom aide in your school at the time and I'd swing by your lonesome lunch table to ask how your day was going. You never seemed perturbed to be separated from your classmates. I wondered even then how that isolation might affect your personality development. It was probably on my mind because I felt highly conscious of the emotional distance between my own peers and me, which was a riddle of chicken or egg—did I struggle to relate to people my age because I was a straight edge punk rock kid, or had I become one because it had always been so hard to relate to people? It's one of the many ties that bind us, Gyasi. We're together in our separateness and have been for a long time.

The Black Momba likes to recount a confrontation she had with one of your primary school teachers. The teacher had written in a mid-quarter progress report that you didn't play particularly well with others. To substantiate the charge, she cited an example of how you behaved during free time. While other students rushed to get their stations of choice first, you waited until all your peers had settled into their various perches in the classroom. Then you went to the corner of the room with the fewest students and played by yourself. The Black Momba didn't buy that this avoidant behavior was problematic. She pushed back on the teacher's conviction that your aversion to group socialization was something that needed correcting. For a black boy, she insisted, it was adaptive. I was heeding similar instincts in practicing straight edge—seeking out the least populous territory within a subculture and settling it like a frontier. We both use solitude as an aegis, and I can't help but be ambivalent about that. I'm not sure that I want to encourage you to glide forever along the perimeter of your own life, but doing so has certainly extended mine.

In the history of my unfortunate, punk-inspired fashion choices, a black jean jacket on which I'd sloppily written "straight edge xxx" with one of those hokey, glitter paint pens would probably be a candidate for the hall of shame. One good thing that came of it, however, was that an aging punk chef who worked at my food service job spotted my jacket hanging in the back of our restaurant and, after connecting me with the garment, made a ritual of repeating the following apocryphal story to me about his adventures as a militant straight edger:

Lucas hovers in a shadowy alcove of a grocery store, stealthy and vigilant as an owl overlooking a placid meadow, mohawked hair streaming gallantly in the October wind like a subversive flag, leather jacket zipped high enough to conceal his unsmiling mouth. His image bears a striking resemblance to the shadowy figure depicted on those neighborhood watch signs that clutter the poles of streetlights and abandoned buildings in urban areas. Looking at him, you feel compelled to superimpose the words "we report all suspicious activities and persons to law enforcement" over his lithe torso. His scornful gaze is directed at the rear entrance of the store, where two employees, young and off-the-clock exultant, loiter with a coterie of friends of roughly high school age, their jocular speech and breezy laughter echoing down the empty alley.

If you weren't watching as closely as Lucas, you might attribute the clouds of smoke that the jovial clique emits to the evening's frosty temperature, rather than the pack of cigarettes they're sharing. Lucas gathers himself to confront the unsuspecting organic grocery workers and their cronies, a keen prickling of imminent violence suffusing his tensed form.

"Drop the smokes," Lucas bellows in a voice like a rumble strip, streaking toward the night revelers at full tilt, an atom bomb carrying innumerous tons of explosive sanctimony. Relishing the ripple of trepidation that darts through the circle of smokers, he stretches out his gnarled, filthy hands, each crudely emblazoned with a trifecta of x's. "Give me the cigs or somebody is getting hospitalized tonight."

"Hate edge!" a hanger-on gasps, a Muggle-born announcing the arrival of Lord Voldemort. Most of the crowd disperses with impressive speed, but a single, gangly, male remains. Chest outstretched, pack of Marlboros in hand, he shoves Lucas's protruding fists back in the direction of their owner.

"Take them from me."

Within a moment as brief as the interim between a drag and exhalation, the gangly boy has paid dearly for his hubris. Suddenly dazed and moaning at an unobstructed view of the mid-autumn constellations, he slowly raises his fingers to the blood leaking copiously from his nose. Standing over him, Lucas leers, lobs a loogie at the humbled teenager's crumpled face.

"It was a pleasure."

The Marlboros slung satisfyingly into the back pocket of his ripped jeans, Lucas scoots off into the darkness to consult the grocery store's dumpster for dinner options. Homeless, unemployed, and shamelessly antisocial, the punk rock lifer would not be amenable to any suggestion that he is merely a parasite of the system. By the logic of his scarcely educated, undernourished, and half-shaven head, tonight's events represented a generous contribution to society.

I traveled to Egypt during one of my last semesters of grad school. I was thirty years old and it was my first time leaving the country. My hosts told me to expect to be identified as a tourist and targeted by beggars and merchants accordingly. When African Americans make their way to what's known as the motherland, the tropes invite us to view the experience as a homecoming. Instead, I felt more conscious of myself as a pampered dweller of the first world traveling to the global south. The last thing I wanted to do was accidentally fall into any of the condescending postures that made my own society's most privileged members so insufferable. I'd sooner be a hapless mark for con artists than a haughty American. It was a relief to learn a hand gesture that meant "no thank you." When panhandlers or street sellers approached me and made their pitches, my hosts instructed me to say *la shukran* while placing my right hand over my heart. If a stranger was calling to me from a distance and my voice couldn't be heard over the din of zooming traffic or the commotion of other pedestrians, just making the hand over heart gesture would communicate something like "Yo, good looking out, but I'm good."

A shorthand for respectful, even appreciative refusal was something that eluded me during my tenure as an American straight edge kid. In my life in the states, turning down a glass of wine, a line of coke, a drag of a cigarette, a hit of the blunt, an offer to hook up was so often taken as an affront. I was not, or at least didn't aspire to be, the defiant do-gooder in one of those "My Anti-Drug" public service campaigns. Though matters of conscience informed my decision to abstain, I had no desire to make anyone else feel like their own decisions to partake were moral failures. I was trying to embody noncompliance that didn't indict those who complied. At parties, I declined favors as nonchalantly as possible, typically only invoking straight edge when "Nah, I'm aight" hadn't worked.

The goal was practice without preaching. There was an irony to the idea that choosing to value my own autonomy was received primarily in terms of how it reflected on other people. I wanted to think for myself. It would undermine the sanctity of that project to deny other people the same right. I think of the body language I resorted to most often on the streets of Cairo as a summation of what straight edge meant to me. The right hand over my heart gesture symbolizes both the sincerity of my commitment to straight edge and a live-and-let-live praxis of it. *La shukran.*

Punk is the first subculture I immersed myself in with the vivid awareness that it was in fact a subculture. It showed me that if the dominant culture was the main thoroughfare, there were likely to be all kinds of side streets and alcoves where none of the main thoroughfare's assumptions were taken as a given. As a teenager, I projected rather than having to constantly undergo the tedious internal calculus I used to make important decisions, it would be far easier to have a settled, unwavering stance on issues of drug use and promiscuous sex. The history and tradition of straight edge merely provided ethos, I figured, for a position that was comically unusual within the circles I ran. The acute insularity of punk culture meant that I was wrong, of course; mentioning that I was straight edge induced far more quizzical expressions than knowing glances. Straight edge became more like vague shorthand for "you can skip me when you're passing around the joint" than a source of validation by way of strength in numbers.

. The invocation of straight edge's traditional symbol of three x's, or even just the reception of the terse whisper "I'm edge" over a crowded bar, functions as a Rorschach. To many, the terminology has no explicit connection to punk rock (a hugely ambiguous term to begin with) but is merely an implicit admission of profound and debilitating wackness. For others, straight edge connotes gang activity, muscled toughs with shaven heads stalking and intimidating cigarette smokers and potheads in the name of some righteous but opaque agenda. Often, even when the general ideological underpinnings are known or explained, there is a tendency to overextend the movement's·rules in the way a befuddled gentile asks a Jewish person if they "can do Thanksgiving."

Acknowledging being straight edge out loud in mixed company has provoked variants of the following:

"So, do you people take aspirin?"

"You don't drink? Are you gay?"

"Can you all drink cola? I mean, caffeine is a dangerous drug, too!"

"Are you like, vaccinated for stuff or is that not allowed?"

Lightning rod that it is, straight edge's most reliable property is its uncanny capacity to cause anger. To many, fasting steadfastly at what some people perceive as the banquet of life is an insult to propriety, to decency, to a rich tradition of impulsive and reckless behavior that has long characterized idealizations of the West, masculinity, and sweet freedom herself. Somewhere along the way the culture of devotion to recreational substance use (and sometimes abuse) began to sustain the presumption that to refrain from those activities is to malign those who indulge in them. I'm often told that I'm fortunate to be an artist because if I were an entrepreneur I'd struggle to connect with other businesspeople without drinking. In my years of trying to stealthily divert conversation away from my teetotaling, what feels like a battalion of strong-jawed dudes with identical haircuts have explained to me that a savvy businessman would never trust someone who doesn't drink.

The first time I was offered a drink I was fourteen, bored to tears in seventh-period computer lab. A white kid I played JV soccer with snuck a couple of Smirnoff Ices in his gym bag and brought it to class. We called him Spock because of his misshapen ears. Spock handed me one of the chilled bottles beneath our desktops and outlined a scenario in which he, myself, and a few other dudes from the team invited our counterparts from the girls' team to have drinks in his basement.

"Just picture it—me, you, Todd, some of the hotter girl players—drinking these and chilling at my house this weekend."

I cast a furtive glance toward the front of the room. The instructor was preoccupied, so I twisted off the top and took a sip.

"It's good, isn't it?" Spock pronounced, smirking. "You can't tell me that's not good."

For reasons unrelated to alcohol specifically, I wasn't inclined to grant him the satisfaction of my approval. This was the same kid, after all, who set the tone for the team's first practice earlier that school year by asking everyone to share their "favorite racist jokes" while we were warming up on the field and waiting for the coaching staff to arrive. The team had only two other visibly nonwhite players, neither of whom took exception to the wantonly offensive humor. When I confronted Spock, he shrugged me off. I was apparently taking things too seriously.

"Relax. If I meant any of these jokes," Spock crowed, "you would already be strung up by your neck from that telephone pole over there." He gestured dramatically across the field and wiggled his eyebrows in emphasis, performing for the guffawing stooges already lining up behind him. Spock turned out to be one of the team's best players. He had the ear and the esteem of our black coach. I didn't want to ride the pine all year so I made sure to reach an uneasy detente with Spock to survive the soccer season. Now he was using alcohol to lure me to a social event that would almost certainly be attended by the same mouth-breathing sidekicks who had been tickled at the thought of lynching me on the soccer field.

This was ninth grade, which meant the hang-sesh that Spock was envisioning would establish key social precedents. Alcohol would become a staple of all the gatherings that popular, athletic students were invited to and mere mortals bemoaned their exclusion from. That year as I mulled the decision to become straight edge, the association between drinking and Spock's clique lingered in my mind. Claiming edge was effectively consolidating an existing ideological gap between myself and those of my peers who thought racist jokes made swell icebreakers. Spock and his acolytes were staking out a zone. He'd already established the tenuous conditions under which I'd be welcome or, really, tolerated. The edge was a line of demarcation between that zone and where I wanted to be.

I gravitated to straight edge quite naively, but it wasn't long before I realized that staying straight edge came with numerous ramifications. From my rigidly spectatorial vantage point, I came to appreciate how integral risky behaviors were to adolescent socialization. I was both pierced and protected by the double straight-edged sword. Being on the outside looking in on so many social rituals heightened the feelings of alienation that drew me to punk rock to begin with. At the same time, it was clear to me that I might otherwise have remedied my loneliness—which preceded and overlapped with my time as a straight edger—in dangerous and perhaps even lethal ways.

It took a while for me to realize that one of the reasons I'm straight edge is because when I was a kid, Joe and I were left in the care of a group of Mom's relatives I referred to as the "cousins by the dozens." Several generations on Mom's side were crammed into a tiny apartment a short metro bus ride from our own. What was a couple more fledgling humans, really, in the squalor of poverty and laissez-faire babysitting? Someone in that house almost certainly sexually abused someone else who lived in that house, and that latter someone else sexually abused me. I'm not sure how long it went on or how often.

Each time it happened, my body would wisely furlough my mind, which floated away and traversed more idyllic scenes—memories of getting croissants at the St. Louis Bread Company, plunging into the ball pit at the local Discovery Zone, leveling a piece of the set with a karate kick during strike after the finale of our parents' plays. Extensive practice at this dissociation eventually made it automatic, a reflex I could not suppress without great effort. For years after, the sight of naked people made my head swim and my stomach churn, first on screens and then in person. Even as an adult, when my conscious mind sought intimacy with cautious enthusiasm, some persistent nether layer regarded sex as an ordeal. It wasn't until my late twenties that I began to connect the dots between these aftershocks and the decision to become straight edge.

In claiming edge I'd found an inconspicuous way to prop an "out of order" sign on my own brain and genitals. The downside to that out of order sign being, of course, that I treated my own sexuality the way you'd regard an elevator labeled with one: I ignored it. With a couple years of therapy, eros eventually became a language I could speak haltingly and with some concentration, but even then, it still felt like light years from being a mother tongue.

Abstaining from drugs, alcohol, and nicotine are the vowels of straight edge, and avoiding promiscuous sex is the "sometimes *y*." Most people who call themselves straight edge reject substance use. Possibly because "promiscuous" or "casual" sex is such a subjective notion, the tenet of straight edge that pertains to sex is often the most negotiable. It seems likely I took that plank of the platform more seriously than most. You're probably familiar, Gyasi, with the dramatic principle that states "if you say in the first chapter that there is a rifle hanging on the wall, in the second or third chapter it absolutely must go off."[2] Playwright Anton Chekhov proffered the adage as a way to emphasize that a story is best served by the elimination of any and all nonessential elements. Who would guess that gravitating to punk might help me render the most untoward element of my childhood in strikethrough font? Straight edge provided me with a means of unloading and peacefully disassembling Chekhov's gun. Abuse and a litany of nonconsensual encounters that crudely rehearsed the abuse introduced the gun, let it gleam under the stage lights and beckon menacingly at a future in which some dastardly character might empty its clip. Knowing that the person who originally victimized me was victimized in a similar fashion herself, I was and remain keen to disrupt the chain of sordid inheritance. I can't count the times I have covertly Googled the adult outcomes of childhood sexual abuse. I thank my lucky stars that straight edge has scuttled the most explosive possible consequences.

I've wondered if we can count Brand New's leading man, singer, guitarist, and disgraced emo deity Jesse Lacey, who is the author of the seventh track on your mixtape, as among the survivors who in turn make survivors of others.

Lacey and Brand New rose to prominence in the early 2000s, when their baroquely long-winded song titles and brooding lyricism captured the hearts of the LiveJournal generation. "Sic Transit Gloria . . . Glory Fades" is the second single from their cheekily named *Deja Entendu* (already heard). The song was something I had definitely not ever heard—a depiction of unwanted sex from a male perspective. The average listener has the option to succumb to the hypnosis of Garrett Tierney's hauntingly catchy bass line and let the lyrics fade into white noise. The discomfiting narrative Lacey unspools about a boy too unsure of himself to halt a sexual encounter with an overzealous partner chimed so neatly with my own experiences that I couldn't tune it out.

What's brilliant about "Sic Transit" is that it straddles the maddeningly thin line between what's sexy and what's scary. In the verses, the strut of the rhythm section is both sultry and threatening. The sudden onslaught of overdriven guitars in the heart-pounding chorus approximates an orgasm—or is it a panic attack? "Sic Transit" conjures the somatic dimensions of when a would-be amorous overture activates a fight-or-flight response. Game recognizes game; does traumatized detect its likeness too? I'm hesitant to assume that any given Brand New song is autobiographical, but it certainly sounds like Lacey knows of which he strums.

Two women accused Lacey of sexual misconduct in 2017, shortly after the release of the band's fifth and final record, *Science Fiction*. His accusers alleged that the events took place fifteen years earlier, when the two women were in their teens and Lacey was in his twenties.[3] Lacey issued a vague public apology via the band's Facebook, in which he admitted to struggling with sex addiction in the past and acknowledged having undergone treatment for it long before the allegations against him became public.

If "Sic Transit" is, in fact, autobiographical, then the events Lacey's accusers describe perhaps represent Chekhov's rifle going off in the second and third chapters, the combustive outcomes straight edge has spared me from. As we've talked about before, Gyasi, there's this assumed predestination to male sexuality in general, even for those who are not survivors. When it comes to sex, we men often prefer to frame ourselves as passive adherents of the rigid programming begat by some rugged hunter-gatherer ancestor. The edge showed me that I could and should act as my sexuality's charioteer. Whatever imprint the trauma may have had, I could still be guided by scruples rather than impulses.

There's an excellent GIF of Tahj Mowry, in character as Disney's *Smart Guy*, gaping off into the distance of what looks like a high school lunchroom before cupping his hand and raising it to his face so as to block his peripheral vision.

With eyes darting back and forth, he winces and tilts his body away from the direction of whatever cringe-worthy sight has unsettled him. Can an image be pithy? It's a cogent encapsulation of both of our temperaments, down to the cafeteria backdrop. You've probably seen Internet users rummage up the Mowry GIF to communicate awkwardness or discomfort. To me, there's more. I see it as what some psychologists call "embodied cognition," a representation of a visceral experience that shapes abstract thought. In the GIF, Mowry is doing physically what you and I do philosophically—fading back into the pocket of our interiority to insulate the self from unfavorable terrain. I imagine that the Smart Guy is leaning into the void and wielding it like Captain America's shield.

The Tahj Mowry GIF makes me think of "portable seclusion," a term the anthropologist Hanna Papanek coined to describe veiled Muslim women in Pakistan. There's a fairly relentless orientalism to how burkas are understood in the West. They're mostly construed as symbols of demure subservience, so I was intrigued by this reframing of the burka as a kind of social mosquito netting or a cage for separating sharks.

I sometimes ponder a possible correspondence between choosing to be a straight edge African American and choosing to be a veiled woman in the Middle East. It's a link that came to mind during the early stages of the COVID-19 pandemic, when US Surgeon General Jerome Adams singled out Americans of color to stop drinking, smoking, and doing drugs.[4] After briefly acknowledging the social and economic factors that have caused the virus to hit black and Latinx communities disproportionately hard, Adams made a heel turn and used his bully pulpit to scold us for our alleged vices. The implication was that our heightened vulnerability to the virus is a result of personal failings rather than structural realities. Adams's soundbite was more likely a way of stoking the right-wing masses than a credible, if gratuitous, attempt to inspire communities of color to buck up. Heeding the surgeon general's call would require no change in my behavior, but I didn't read Adams's comments and mop my brow in relief. I have no illusions that being straight edge will necessarily spare me from a painful, solitary death in an overcrowded hospital as helpless nurses look on in despondent resignation. Adams offers neither practical nor moral insurance. Being substance-free provides me a modicum of portable seclusion, of distance from undue influence or surveillance, but it doesn't mean I have any more virtue than anyone else. Yet it could appear at first glance that Adams and I are on the same side.

The decision to veil can likewise register to some as a capitulation to the male gaze, a feckless concession to the forces that dehumanize and confine women. In her essay "The Muslim Woman: The Power of Images and the Danger of Pity," anthropologist Lila Abu-Lughod argues that this reading overlooks veiled women's agency and self-determination. Abu-Lughod points out that Muslim women make decisions about their attire and their faith that may superficially appear to align with patriarchy but that are nonetheless assertions of selfhood and avowals of individual values.[5] Freedom from domination can't merely be a matter of having the right to be the polar opposite of your oppressor. It seems to me, Gyasi, that such freedom must mitigate the oppressor's primacy as a frame of reference. In its most absolute form, freedom should allow for your actions and those of your antagonists to be fully orthogonal pursuits.

I would like to think that Abu-Lughod's argument reflects my own relationship with straight edge. Resisting domination can manifest in a variety of ways and can sometimes uncomfortably resemble acquiescing to it.

Looking back, I can recognize the formative experiences that shaped my particular values. During periods when our parents were either both working day jobs or tied up with producing plays, I spent my weekday afternoons and evenings at my elementary school's extended day program. Extended day was like its own pedagogical subcontinent. It was school's faintly hipper alter ego. The counselors, who were on average significantly younger than our teachers, aspired to be less like stern taskmasters than cool older siblings. Study hall was one of the primary activities used to pass the time until parents with jobs that ended at 5 p.m. could retrieve their kids. The last thing children under twelve want to do immediately after they get out of six hours of instruction is start their homework, so Big Brad, my extended day counselor, got creative. He bribed us into submission with the promise of what he called "brain powder."

He'd lumber around the room evaluating how committed each student was to their studying or reading pantomime. If the student seemed worthy, he'd shake a few lumps of Jell-O powder into their outstretched hands as the student squirmed with delight. Lots of us would goof off for most of study hall until we saw Big Brad peeling the seal off the Jell-O box, at which point we'd hasten to look busy, like little factory workers overhearing the supervisor's foreboding footsteps. Big Brad would initially withhold brain powder from those who took this tack but then circle back periodically to give them further opportunities to earn a treat.

I was a child, but I still wanted to believe I was a person with free will and a backbone and—I don't know—dignity? It made my skin crawl that a handful of sugar and food coloring could be leveraged as a form of power. Every time I felt Big Brad's burly shadow approaching, I kept my eyes fixed squarely on the book in my hand. And when he reached out to reward me with a pitiful smattering of brain powder, I gently waved him off without looking up. It was one of the few experiences I had where thwarting the mechanics of subordination didn't lead to censure. It led to respect. After this same pattern unfolded for several study halls in a row, Big Brad realized I couldn't be bought with fodder for wobbly desserts. From then on, things that were "directions" for the other kids became more like "suggestions" in my case, ideas for activities that Big Brad would ask me what I thought about.

There were racial overtones at play as well. Extended day was a program at an expensive private school with a negligible black population. The few black students who were present were, for the most part, relatively wealthy. Almost none trekked from the side of town I would return to when Baba came to pick me up each evening. I was aware that even the most inconsequential choices I made would be viewed as a referendum on a tawdry underclass. Which is where the line between basic self-determination and tacit endorsement of respectability politics blurs uncomfortably for me. Gyasi, I'm not saying I was Ruby Bridges here, but every instinct told me that being brought to heel by some white man with raw gelatin on the tip of his finger was a betrayal of the block. The development of this emotional muscle memory surely informed my receptivity to straight edge.

For a typical punk fan, being straight edge is an extension of fandom, a way to become distinct from a larger peer group in order to secure access to a smaller, more exclusive one. For an upwardly mobile black kid, going edge is the embodiment of former US congressman Paul Ryan's wet dream. The largely unmarked irony of punk's angst, nihilism, and suspicion of authority is that it is a movement that in most of its American iterations has been led by people who benefit most from the status quo. Despite the prevailing narratives about race and rock 'n' roll, punk's disaffection with rules, norms and the over-determinacy of social roles is an unease black folks are exceedingly familiar with. As a young black male keenly tuned in to the legal and social perils that come with my territory, straight edge is perhaps more intuitive and practically useful to me as a lifestyle blueprint than to punk rock's white male ruling class. Committing to straight edge in my teens was a logical byproduct of our parents' having instilled in me an appreciation for the precariousness of my freedom, peace, and health in a society that is consistently determined to see black people as dangerous criminals.

Despite our parents' initial wide-eyed bewilderment at my fascination with punk rock, by being straight edge I was still more or less emulating the example of what I'd seen at home. Each of our parents grew up in households with cigarette smokers. Both Mom and Baba decided as children never to wreak the same havoc on the lungs of their own progeny. To boot, early experiences with alcoholic relatives in both our mother's and our father's extended families caused them to shun drinking entirely as well. The Black Momba's idea of a wild night is when she mixes a splash of apple juice into her and Baba's glasses of ginger ale. These choices and tastes, in our mother's eyes, were not merely incidental to her success in overcoming being an unwed teenage mother and eventual Northwestern University dropout born and raised in working-class East St. Louis, Illinois. Bizarrely, my attraction to straight edge may have as much to do with trite adages about "being twice as good to get half as far" as my enduring love for Gorilla Biscuits albums.

That those adages dovetail so neatly with the doctrine of conservatives like Ryan, a man who sees disproportionate poverty and incarceration among African Americans as chiefly attributable to black pathology, is evidence of the degree to which even progressive black folks have internalized the worldview that posits black dysfunction as a cause and not a symptom of systemic inequity. I inevitably took on being straight edge with different baggage than many of my counterparts in the overwhelmingly white local punk scene I was introduced to as a ninth grader.

Chugging bottles of Yoo-hoo at parties in place of the more popular beverage choices made me an iconoclast among revelers, but it also maintained a barrier between myself and what talk radio gasbags would call the black community's "culture problem." The possibility that straight edge's positive impact on my life might provide any kind of implicit validation of the mostly absurd precepts of GOP sociology is unsettling. Still, rejecting self-destructive habits provides only limited insulation from the machinery of a system designed to expedite that destruction for you.

Refraining from drinking, drugs, and approaching sex as a conquest did not imbue my life with newfound value, but it has helped me to remain observant of my life's inherent value while living in a country that insists I am deluded.

In the wake of the unceremonious executions of Kayla Moore, Michelle Cusseaux, Shelly Frey, and others, black folks have disputed the relevance of respectability politics in preserving black lives in the face of a white supremacist culture and an increasingly militarized police force. The growing visibility of similar deaths has cast doubt that being an exemplary citizen, dressing in attire white people deem innocuous, or cooperating with police are any kind of bulwark against the corrosive ethnocentrism that is still an organizing force in American life.

But even though it was not a conscious selling point for me, the sanitizing influence that being straight edge has had on the specifics of my biography would at the very least complicate efforts to cast me as "no angel,"[6] as the *New York Times* infamously described Michael Brown, the unarmed teenager shot and killed August 2014 in Ferguson, Missouri. As I reached my middle and late twenties, I grew increasingly ambivalent toward edge, but not because I became tired of ordering cranberry juice at bars or failing to grasp the subtleties of stoner humor. It was more that the growing pains I underwent as an upstart writer, student, and citizen compelled me to consider for the first time whether I'd gone for the okey-doke, whether the seductiveness of punk's swaggering contrarianism had tricked me into trying to punch my ticket to prosperity by sheer force of moral rectitude. What didn't kill me made me stronger on the job market.

American Idiolect

An Annotation of Fefe Dobson's
"Stupid Little Love Song"

During move-in week of my sophomore year in college, I loitered in my dorm lobby, offering my (scarcely) muscled assistance to passersby. Arms spread in a box-lifting pantomime, I flashed a warm smile at several indifferent coeds before one bubbly, fresh-faced junior returned serve. Having just transferred that semester to our Midwestern liberal arts college the same as I had, she mentioned looking forward to the winter because she was from California and had rarely experienced snow.

"I'm from right outside Washington, DC," I told her. "So I guess I don't feel like you're missing much."

She narrowed eyes as blue as the Pacific she'd left behind. "But don't you like seasons?"

"Well, I'm nondogmatic on fall. But I'm unequivocally anti-winter."

The pleasingly symmetrical features twisted cartoonishly.

"Nondogmatic?" She echoed, as if I'd veered jaggedly into an extraterrestrial tongue. "You're une-*what* about winter?"

"Oh, I just meant—" I began.

"Whoa," she gasped. "Did your parents sign you up for *talk smart* classes when you were a kid?"

"Uh, nah . . . do those exist?"

"My parents definitely didn't," she said breathlessly. "I can't talk like that."

I stared, dumbfounded, thinking of that devastating George Bernard Shaw quote: "The single biggest problem with communication is the illusion that it has taken place." It seemed inelegant to explain that my rhetorical style—needless to say, a signature feature of my macking approach—wasn't a pretension or a product of intensive study. I'd gone to a mediocre public high school like everyone else, and while my SAT verbal score was far better than its quantitative counterpart, I'd staked my college admission essay on the claim that my lackluster total had "shambolic charm." Worse, to say that I talked that way all the time without any particular effort because it was fun and it pleased me would be to sound like I was congratulating myself. And here was the best part, Gyasi: I'd devised the sentences in question in the manner I did mainly in the interest of brevity, to make a nuanced point in a minimum of words. When your most acclaimed vehicle for wooing promising young women is talking, you learn pretty quickly that verbiage is a virtue only when used in moderation.

Being reluctantly yoked smack-dab in the generation of telephones smarter than people, it was easy to ascertain that any faith in the common human's attention span was profoundly misplaced. Often, if I'm talking to anyone other than a shrink or my momma, their willingness to halt their own blathering to affect the pretense of listening to me is draining forebodingly from their face, like descending numbers on an NBA shot clock that redden as they approach zero. I've evolved to try to pack as much substance into as few syllables as I can in that blessed twenty-four-second window between my co-converser taking a breath and their inevitable decision to eclipse me with their own words. I was aware of all of these considerations as I chatted up the buoyant pixie from the Best Coast. Juggling them was integral to the code of light, ingratiating conversation that portended romantic success in those days. One momentary lapse of attention had dashed my hopes with a thud. As you'll no doubt discover on campus next fall, undergraduate macking is like running for office. Cultivating the ideal proportion of sincerity and artifice is vital to the success of your stump speech. Like a policy wonk trotting out a clunky pop culture reference, I'd too quickly revealed myself as someone you'd rather borrow lecture notes from than have a beer with.

I was still carrying the SoCal transplant's box of beachy, hippie trinkets and posters from Wes Anderson movies when in walked a rival more adept at interfacing with the right code. I could only gape helplessly as the tall, waifish Adrien Brody lookalike swooped in to usurp me.

"Sup, biddy?" he muttered casually through his sharp, alpine nose. He produced a joint. "You wanna go outside and hit this skrizzle with me?"

While having skrizzle in your pocket is always a considerable advantage, watching the carefree pair disappear into the campus woods together didn't make me feel outdone exactly. I felt more like a self-styled pinch, dab, and smidgen chef who maybe should have used a measuring cup just this once.

A few years earlier, I trekked to Baltimore with my four wide-eyed bandmates in tow to put my first full-length record to tape. For months, we'd been fine-tuning our collection of a dozen or so three-and-a-half-minute pop punk songs, and entering the studio with then producer du jour Paul Leavitt seemed to us a plum opportunity to make something indelible. As the band's guitarist, chief lyricist, and resident literary nerd, I had agonized endlessly over every hook and cranny of the words and melodies. At twenty, I was inexperienced enough to expect that through the force of sheer will I could vanquish the prevailing understanding of pop punk as thoughtless, juvenile encomiums to fast food restaurants and bubblegum. While my bandmates certainly didn't share my determination to shatter unbecoming stereotypes about the musical tradition in which we had chosen to operate, everyone paid little attention to the intricacies of my writing on the new album until we'd arrived at the studio. As we listened to the playback of our frontman's best take, it wasn't my bandmates who piped up first but the engineer, Paul Leavitt's brassy assistant, Kory Gable. He frowned as our vocalist's sparkling baritone trumpeted from the oversized speakers more expensive than a year's worth of my rent.

I'm undercover on your coast
You're sailing his sheets
My lookout utters "there she blows!"
I swashbuckle streets
And my cutlass cuts lasses
with coquettish eyelashes
And we'll scatter all your ashes
All across the seven seas.

Kory nudged the pause button and began laughing.

"Did he just say 'my cutlass cuts lasses with cokeheadish eyelashes'?"

The band's other guitar player, Greg, looked to me. Our bass player, Rory, peered quizzically at Greg.

"I always thought it was 'cokeheadish,'" Greg chortled.

"*Is* it 'cokeheadish'?" Rory wondered.

"It's 'coquettish,'" I enunciated, straining not to sound like a smug spelling bee emcee. I turned to Kory. "You know, like flirtatious, or . . . coyly inviting, I guess?"

Kory smirked.

"You can't use a word like that in a song. That's like an SAT word."

"Is that a rule?" I riposted. A keen defensiveness indebted to a lifetime of having this same conversation swelled up inside me. "Would you tell Ben Gibbard he couldn't use 'coquettish' in a song? Would you say that to Max Bemis?" I was flattering myself by name-checking the two wordsmiths who fronted Death Cab for Cutie and Say Anything, respectively.

Kory was flummoxed.

"That's different because Ben Gibbard and Max Bemis play smart music. You guys play pop *punk*," he declared, emphasizing his final syllable as if it were a synonym for "infantile moron." That hasty dismissal of the very aesthetic I was deliberately trying to develop—in thoughtful opposition to the dominant assumptions about the genre—ended up setting the tone for the rest of the recording experience. Kory didn't entertain the possibility that our music *could be* smart. He didn't attempt to rationalize precisely why elevated language didn't belong in the world of crunchy guitars and soaring choruses. He only allowed that something about the blurring of what he believed were distinct spheres unsettled him. After the album was finished, we'd hear through the Baltimore pop punk scene's teeming gossip network that Kory and Paul would hesitate to work with us again. To the seasoned duo's ears, our band "wasn't bad at all. Just weird, but really fucking weird." Arguing with Kory never really felt like debating an idea with a person. It seemed more like returning fire at an entire culture. It's probably illustrative of a dishearteningly pervasive pattern in my life as a communicator, a pattern I suspect would be familiar to you, too, Gyasi, if you ever ventured to open your mouth in public.

By now I'm accustomed to being told that I'm speaking at the wrong altitude for a given discourse, that the words I reach for automatically either stoop or tower too dramatically for the setting. No part of this debate has followed me more doggedly than its racial element. The assumed divide between black and white speech is a reductive, sophistic notion I have bristled against as far back as I can remember. Certainly, one's sociopolitical position can influence the ways in which one engages with language and the kinds of thoughts that demand urgent expression. Conceiving of racialized speech in binary opposition, however, is depressingly lazy and uncritical, not least because doing so presupposes that the two camps communicate monolithically.

Growing up as a budding word enthusiast in urban North St. Louis, I was subject to code policing from all sides. The nature of my early life made it difficult for a binary understanding of language and identity to compute. My zip code encompassed an overwhelmingly black, poverty-ravaged maelstrom of gang violence and drug mercantilism. By contrast, the elite private elementary school I rode two city buses to get to every morning in the city's Central West End was an incubator for the children of the white elite. Each milieu presented its own navigational challenges for me, the son of two bohemian Northwestern University dropouts who ran their own theater company from our rickety kitchen table in one of the nation's most murderous ghettos.

Even with only a nascent grasp of the traumatic history that underlined it, I was hip to the condescension at play when well-meaning white authority figures at school couldn't stop marveling that I could "speak so well!" But I was equally exasperated when backyard arguments with the neighbor-hood kids would inevitably culminate with someone lobbing the charge that I "talked like a white boy," as if no betrayal could be more heinous. The message was clear: you're a sub-altern, kid, and we expect you to talk like it.

Accusations of inauthentic blackness and white amaze-ment at my formulation of coherent paragraphs both struck me as unfounded. I was reluctant to accept the premise from which these syllogisms were generated. The avalanche of books that overwhelmed my household's cramped, ram-shackle living room provided confirmation that there was no shortage of staggeringly eloquent brown people and that many of them and their gifts of gab had played pivotal roles in American history. Handwritten reproductions of James Wel-don Johnson poems were scotch-taped to the jagged-edged walls of our dusty, crumbling hallways. Worn, hand-me-down alphabet magnets pinned Marcus Garvey quotes to the refrig-erator door. Between daily jaunts through the concrete jun-gle and casual exposure to the literary tastes of our aesthete parents, my first nine years were a comprehensive overview of the alleged genus of black verbiage. There was no credible reason to view as standard the speech proclivities of the swag-gering Crip across the street who offered Joe crack every day.

I even chafed when our parents would try to placate me with the suggestion that I just needed to learn to be more "cul-turally bilingual." It was frustrating that two people whose daily activities flew in the face of this mythic dichotomy seemed to validate it even as they urged me to transcend it.

Doing homework in my bedroom, I'd often overhear Mom concocting songs and dialogue for the musicals she produced with Baba. Assessing them aloud in her own voice, she'd thunder with august Shakespearean diction one moment and slur streetwise colloquialisms the next, often while inhabiting the same character. Telling me I needed to be schooled in two different, color-coded tongues nettled me in a deep and abiding way. It was like saying that the complexity and variety of the language I observed every day was something I'd only imagined.

I didn't want to be "culturally bilingual" because I rejected the notion that one style of speech corresponded unilaterally with one group, or that its opposite belonged exclusively to a separate one. The fellow ghetto dwellers I knew from the block did not, as far as I could tell, constitute "a people." It seemed a stretch that everyone struggling in theaters of inner city warfare—from the teenage crackheads in the abandoned house two blocks down to the retired homeowners next door who'd been married thirty years—shared a culture that could be understood as a coherent whole. It wasn't only that the categories used to silo language felt inadequate. The very inclination to use speech for sequestering didn't smell quite right. To use words in the service of solidifying divisions, or to view them as resources to which only a select group are entitled, is to fundamentally misapprehend their magic. But I understood the territoriality other people seemed to have about language, even if I didn't relate to it. If knowledge is power, then words are levers for its manipulation.

In first grade, a babysitter got me out of her hair by cuing up Spike Lee's *Malcolm X*, a film I barely understood but found transfixing nonetheless. The movie crystallized the relationship between power and eloquence. Malcolm's transition from petty crook to magnetic leader and orator required more than the abandonment of conk and zoot suits. His superhero origin hinged, in part, on the cultivation of an agile tongue, a mastery of talk both plebeian and patrician. Upon returning home from the babysitter's house one evening, I announced my intention to make like Detroit Red and read and hand copy the dictionary word for word. I wanted to possess as many words as possible and to deploy them with Malcolm's discernment. At seven years old, I barely made it past "abrupt," but the short-lived aspiration left a lasting imprint.

I went on to find another model in the wisdom of an animated dog. To the accompaniment of jaunty horn stabs and rollicking piano licks, Billy Joel and Malcolm X seemed to be in conversation with one another. Joel voices Dodger, a streetwise terrier in Disney's 1988 musical Dickens adaptation, *Oliver and Company*. The swaggering canine is a strategic injection of irreverent cool in an otherwise wholesome entry in the Disney canon. Dodger's signature number is "Why Should I Worry?" an up-tempo banger in which he boasts of his panoramic familiarity with his city and the elegant negotiation of its nuances. When Dodger croons, "One minute I'm in Central Park / then I'm down on Delancey Street / From the Bow'ry to St. Marks / There's a syncopated beat," I'm reminded of my childhood fluctuation between unlike zones, my own burgeoning awareness of the subtle correspondences between each. On scholarship in the Central West End, I learned the ropes of private school life alongside white kids from families wealthy enough to pay the sticker price. Then I returned home to the land of fistfights and food stamps in North St. Louis, sopping it all up like sauce overflow on a plate of Baba's barbecued tofu.

Dodger expounds on his grasp of the multivarious in the second verse: "The rhythm of the city / Boy, once you get it down / Then you can own this town / You can wear the crown." Like Malcolm, Dodger's command of varying terrain is central to his power. The rub lies in his adherence to a unifying syncopation. His is a dance defined by fluid motion through liminal space, and the choreography is an intuitive fit for someone of my own beginnings, not to mention yours.

In the tune's irresistible chorus, Dodger celebrates himself as adroit blender of the urban and urbane.

I got street savoir faire.

Over the years I've whistled that hook under my breath like a mantra. There are so many things I like about it, from its valuation of language as a precious commodity to its playful confidence. But it's the concept of "street savoir faire" that I've been most attracted to. The phrase always seemed like a hint, a clue to where I wanted to go with words. The inviting sibilance of the phrase belies its joining of two ideas with opposing connotations. In those three words I hear the harmony between the pedestrian and the aristocratic. Stark, earthly concrete kissed with Francophone refinement and finesse. Street savoir faire feels to me like a way around the limitations of "code switching," a beacon toward something more like code *blurring* or *smearing.*

I'm still indebted to that four-legged sage now. I grew to be invested in writing and speech that complicates or challenges prevailing views of the world. To me, even the most casual kinds of talking and writing have always been critical fronts of a broader deconstructionist project. As an alternative to being culturally bilingual, I opted for what I've come to call "code queering." I landed on "queer" as the verb for this approach to words because of the term's pause-giving properties, its multivalence, its status as reclaimed slur, its transgressive effect. I define code queering as the use of language to defy, revise, or undermine prescriptive ideas about speaking and writing.

"Queerness is disidentification, which would mean that queer writing also moves counter to normative forms," says Darnell L. Moore, writer and managing editor of the *Feminist Wire.*[1] "Queer writing is more fluid than fixed, more disruptive than appeasing. To me, queer writing need not be written by so-named queers, but are forms of writing that refuse to be addressed by conventional writing standards that are shaped by racist, classist and ableist and imperialist legacies that we write and identify, if we are brave enough, as writers."

Kathleen Hanna, punk icon and former front woman of the radical feminist quartet Bikini Kill, is a writer who has proven to be brave enough to flout such legacies. Hanna made a name for herself in the early '90s as a fiery performer and wry provocateur, raising feminist consciousness in the male-dominated Pacific Northwest punk scene and playing a prominent role in the riot grrrl movement. "We just tried to take feminist stuff we read in books and then filter it through a punk rock lens," the musician has said of her band. An unexpected wrinkle to Hanna's rhetorical persona is her signature Valley girl accent. She combines the eloquence of a gender studies professor with the affect of one of Cher Horowitz's cronies in *Clueless*. It was watching Hanna's contemporaries describe her impact in *The Punk Singer*, a 2013 documentary detailing her life and career, that precipitated my eureka moment about code queering.

In the film, when Corin Tucker of Sleater-Kinney does her impression of a young Hanna, she shakes girlishly as if animated in Squigglevision. "Here I am, and I'm going to talk *like this*," Tucker says in character. "And I'm going to sound like a Valley girl and what I have to say is actually totally brilliant and you have to take me seriously."[2]

A cut to an interview with Bratmobile vocalist Allison C. Wolfe reinforces the sentiment. "It goes to show that you can be . . . some Valley girl and you can still be smart and still have feminist ideals and you still should be listened to," Wolfe says.[3]

Hanna's inflection, while genuine, functions as part of her performance. Her critiques of misogyny and sexual violence are deepened by the cadence with which she delivers them. By forcing her audience to contend with their surprise at hearing someone drop science in a Valley girl accent, Hanna exposes the fatuity of the ditz stereotype. The substance of the Bikini Kill singer's famous credo—"grrrls to the front!"—is enhanced by the style used to present it. Her incisive command of the microphone is a subversion of all the faulty justifications for confining women to the margins in punk and beyond.

The effect of this performance relies on a queering of codes—using the rhythms of the "airhead" to elucidate the ideas of the academic. In Hanna, I felt I had an ideological compatriot, an encouraging case study for code queering's efficacy.

More affirmation of the practice's viability came when I stumbled upon an essay I discuss earlier: anthropologist Elizabeth Chin's 1999 "Ethnically Correct Dolls: Toying with the Race Industry," which I read in a gender studies class during my senior year in college. In the essay, Chin suggests that the children's resourcefulness in the absence of black Barbie dolls was best understood as a practice of "race-queering."[4]

She cites the photographs she took during her study that "showed, over and over again, black girls with white dolls whose hair had been elaborately braided, twisted or styled in ways racially marked as black." Instead of seeing the apparent race of the white Barbies as barriers, these girls brought the toys nonchalantly into their own worlds. Rather than feeling constrained to a particular kind of play with the doll because of the doll's racialized appearance, the black children effectively queered the categories toymakers assumed were binding.

Their form of queering is a powerful form of resistance but striking in its simplicity: denying the legitimacy of a construct by not behaving in a way that's beholden to it. Chin's working definition of the word "queering" is "the bending, twisting and flipping of apparently real or natural or accepted social states."

"Embodied in these children's activities is a profound recognition that race is not only socially constructed but has potential to be imaginatively reconstructed," Chin writes. This imaginative reconstruction and queering of consensus categories was an enterprise I'd long undertaken with talk, and recognized in Kathleen Hanna's performance as well. The term "code switching" never sat right with me because "codes" themselves are real or accepted modes that reinforce hierarchies. Naming one variant of English the "proper" one and another variant something like "African American vernacular speech," reinforces a value-laden understanding of difference that usually props up the same tired stereotypes.

I credit little-known Canadian singer-songwriter Fefe Dobson with achieving the catchiest, most spirited example of code queering in a punk rock tune. Her "Stupid Little Love Song" is an imaginative reconstruction of the narrative possibilities of a code that has generally served as an outlet for white male disaffection. Allow me to indulge my inner Rob Gordon for a moment: the artistically crafted mixtape is like a poem. Fefe's emergence on yours, Gyasi, is the volta. If her name registers as a curveball among the household names that make up the majority of your mixtape tracklisting, she's an equally aberrant figure within punk annals in general.

Around the time you were born in 2001, brick-and-mortar record stores were commonplace. People still mostly thought of music as a physical commodity you paid money for and held in your hand. Blossoming art nerd that I was, Borders Books and Music was a highlight of all of my customary teenage trips to the mall. Instant musical gratification was not yet in my horizon of expectation. Napster was only a few years old and Kazaa, which had begun to overshadow it, was so incredibly slow on our family's dial-up Internet that stealing songs that took hours to download felt like more of a hardship than begging Mom for the fourteen bucks it would take to buy the whole record. As a result, the listening stations inside Borders were an oasis. Across from the aisles upon aisles of now vestigial compact discs, you'd find a row of LCD screens, each equipped with a pair of headphones. The listener could select from a menu of complete albums and sample their album of choice right there in the store. I'm not sure what hormonal calculus compelled me to select Fefe Dobson's self-titled debut record. I'm tempted to chalk it up to destiny.

The opening track, "Stupid Little Love Song" was a critical juncture in my punk rock awakening. I was Edna Pontellier and "Stupid Little Love Song" was a piano sonata by Mademoiselle Reisz. The sledgehammer opening riff landed in my brain as if a void, contoured to its exact sonic qualities, had been waiting there all my life. The chord progression is reminiscent of Minor Threat, but Dobson's sassy, megaphone-effected ad-libs are more indebted to the spoken asides in Christina Aguilera's "Genie in a Bottle." Where Aguilera's breathy pseudo-rap went "My body's saying let's go / But my heart is saying no," Dobson augments her chorus with the couplet "three chords and a microphone / hip-hop and rock n roll." As the kick and snare drums seemed to lunge from the speakers to nip at my earlobes, Fefe's haughty, heavily eye-shadowed brown face stared back at me from the glowing LCD screen. The cultural novelty of what I was seeing and hearing struck me instantly. Here was a charismatic black girl unselfconsciously annexing and repurposing a series of genre tropes that were the traditional domain of white men— and doing so with a magnetism and panache that made the combination feel completely intuitive. It called to mind the scene in *Men in Black* where a preening Will Smith dons the iconic outfit for the first time, looks at Tommy Lee Jones and says, "You know what the difference is between me and you?" before answering his own question with "I make this look good." Fefe was an uninvited guest to the punk party (which is forever a black T-shirt affair), but she'd disarmed security with a wink and a blown kiss and all of a sudden become the life of it.

I found "three chords and a microphone" to be a pithy synthesis of hip-hop's and punk rock's key ingredients. I loved the idea of aestheticizing a scrappy, homespun approach to making subversive music and was especially impressed that a Top 40–friendly artist on a major label managed to retain that sensibility on a big budget production like Dobson's debut. I even appreciated that punk and hip-hop both privileged raw inventiveness over virtuosity. But I wasn't sure there was anything hip-hop about "Stupid Little Love Song." The reference to hip-hop actually struck me as discordant, pandering even. I don't need to tell you that hip-hop and blackness are often falsely represented as perfectly coextensive. This is probably connected to how hip-hop is usually discussed as if it's an insurgent cultural movement rather than something that has been thoroughly co-opted and monetized by the authors of the status quo it purports to challenge. Rap music is so overwhelmingly popular that it is the preferred accompaniment of American youth culture, but because it's coded as inflexibly black, it's treated as an innately transgressive mode. A stray Black Star or Public Enemy album made its way into my teenage rotation, but hip-hop's ubiquity made it seem like it belonged less to me than to the norm calibrated masses. The backdrop to my Come to Fefe moment was the rigid power structure of an integrated public high school. Hip-hop dominated the stereos and wardrobes of popular black kids and popular white kids alike. It was impossible to see hip-hop as a vessel for an alternative value system when the upper-middle-class white kids who mocked me because our family didn't own a car could always quote more Big L lyrics from memory than I could. I was also wary of other black people's strained efforts to reference and incorporate hip-hop as proof of their being forward-thinking and with it. To the bewilderment of so many white substitute teachers, I'd groaned loudly when social studies class civil rights documentaries were overlaid with anachronistic hip-hop soundtracks. I'd winced when pre–hip-hop generation poets bent over backward to give props to "conscious" emcees for accepting the torch. Dobson's decision to announce herself as representing some amalgamation of rock and hip-hop was disappointing in the same way. It was as if blackness operating "against type" nonetheless required even the flimsiest mooring to one of its most visible reference points.

These misgivings aside, the song was still something I felt I'd been searching for—an anthem for the itinerants of unlike zones and an exploration of the conundrums that arise from that oscillation. The layer of "Stupid Little Love Song" that resonated most profoundly with my teenage self was the deft inclusion of an acute class consciousness.

As a scrawny black weirdo plucked from the ghetto and dropped unceremoniously into the suburbs, I knew what it was like to share social space with people from tax brackets the stuff of your parents' dreams. My clumsy acclimation to largely white suburbia was the negligible cost of black upward mobility. But hearing a black woman sing about it in a punk context made me feel that my woes—despite being a function of privilege I was pointedly instructed to be grateful for at every turn—were comprehensible and sympathetic. When Dobson notes that she arrived by taxi while her crush arrived by limousine, she describes a contrast that characterized my entire social identity. On one level, I was a literal frequenter of cabs in a neighborhood where everyone drove a car and car ownership held particular social weight. On another, the line spoke to a persistent sensation of class displacement. Even though our family had managed to barnstorm our way into a nexus of prosperity, our upstart means of arrival connoted a cursory belonging at best. Mere proximity to privilege and daily commingling with its beneficiaries did not make one heir to it.

This feeling of disidentification is part and parcel with Dobson's longing for the object of her desire. His pedigree— one of wealth, influence, stability, and access—is not like hers, and her conspicuous awareness of this gulf makes him all the more unreachable—and irresistible. Ultimately, Dobson's street savoir faire is the salve. On paper, the singer knows she can't bring the same material assets to the table that her would-be paramour could, but she recognizes her pluck and creativity as her best bargaining chips and leverages them in song.

"Stupid Little Love Song" is an intervention, a guerilla defacement of the prevailing rules governing black expression. Dobson uses a genre dominated by white men to communicate an experience of compound otherness. The singer's predicament in her choice of genre mirrors the one she finds herself in with her crush. In demonstrating her mastery of the code that is seen as "native" to the dominant class, she underscores the perversity of her exclusion from it. Dobson is the punk equivalent of the Newhallville girls who twist traditionally black hairstyles on to the pates of their white Barbie dolls. I revisit "Stupid Little Love Song" periodically as a blueprint for both code and race queering. It's as spunky and undeniable as any Ramones song and likely to appeal to any fan of the tradition the Ramones are credited for founding. But Dobson proves that the recipe of three chords and a microphone is capacious enough to accommodate a range of experience that the members of the Ramones would likely not have access to.

As Dobson's example demonstrates, code queering is not limited to words. It's finding imaginative ways around and between simply painting a Barbie doll black. It's using spaces of presumed disjuncture to reveal unheralded continuities. Of course, like Dobson and the black girls in New Haven, queering is really just doing what to me seems most obvious. The integrated, multi-textured social landscape I traversed from my childhood onward had always animated me. I'd playfully adopted my own makeshift code alchemy while conscious of the fact that doing so became a performance, an exhibition of my nativity to what others saw as disparate social contexts. Falling back on "cultural bilingualism" would've meant embracing a state of thinking I couldn't see as real or natural at all. Any attempt to short-circuit the power that race exerts on individual expression must first evaluate race's legitimacy as a concept, a step that our parents seemed to skip. Elizabeth Chin's insights spoke to me because she didn't validate the binary thinking behind the phrase "culturally bilingual."

"In looking at the interactions of Newhallville girls and their white dolls, ways of thinking between and outside of bounded racial categories emerge," Chin writes. Speaking in a mode between and outside of bounded categories (racial and otherwise) is precisely the ethos that gave Kory Gable fits, the style that confounded Californian transfer students, the shtick that incited grrrls to riot. For me, it was the only approach that ever made sense.

Cross-pollinating the codes of ivory tower denizens and ordinary straphangers on the bus seems quite natural if public transportation is literally your daily means of getting to and from the lofty bower. Queering the codes becomes a necessary bricolage for reconciling one's constant alternation between tourist and tour guide, interloper and ambassador. The need to create coherence between divides that the world insisted were insoluble became for me both an aesthetic preference and a spiritual affirmation of self.

The most delectable spoken language has always seemed to me deliberately mosaic, a pastiche of unadorned lay speech, stilted poeticism, slang you make up, slang you have overheard, regional aphorisms you inherit from unnameable but essential sources, solecisms that slap like a "proper" syntactical construction could never approximate, cadences that careen suddenly in to the melodic. Code queering is the mode that embraces and demonstrates the sprawling diversity of

English language communication while dovetailing its seemingly divergent strands. It rejects any prescriptive schema of how one's chosen approach to manipulating language corresponds with group membership. It participates only in the politics of pluralism, of hybridity, of multitudes within one. Code queering exposes categories as small-minded impositions that shortchange the observable richness, fluidity, and versatility of group or individual verbal style. It is a synthesis by which a confluence of once segregated discourses is achieved. It is a paradigm that aspires to make livable Walt Whitman's declaration "of every caste and creed am I." It is a both-and aesthetic that draws a winding, luminous throughline to constellate solitary stars. To queer codes effectively is to collect a bouquet comprised of flowers of contrasting sizes and hues—plucked from neighboring fields separated by fences—and through the splendor of that blend imperil all fences. It is to gather lightning and lightning bugs in the same tremulous grasp and brandish the wattage therein to brighten everything in between. Code queering looks upon the supposedly polarized parlances of the street and the academy and traffics in both at once with the gleeful abandon of a toddler who has realized that her crayons scribble as beautifully on the bedroom wall as within the crude coloring book lines they were intended for. Code queering is some revolutionary type shit.

In both private and professional American spheres, diction and grammar are primary instruments of respectability politics. One's ability to string sentences together in accord with a vaunted code is part of how one demonstrates social or occupational worthiness, deservingness or belonging. A lack of facility with what is seen as the "proper" code is sufficient grounds for exclusion and even dehumanization in many cases. As a person who intuitively approaches language like a great, primeval jungle gym, I'm admittedly invested in words in a way that transcends their practical utility. A verbal style that shuffles demurely through social spaces in single file does nothing to heat the blood. I crave the vitality of a code that gallivants, that saunters indecorously, that swings exultantly from chandeliers.

Romanticism aside, granting people such latitude in their speech has clear political ramifications as well. By bringing wreck to the deceptively tidy categories that preserve an unequal status quo, code queering spoils language's appeal as a battleground for moral finger wagging. In the breathless hustle for privilege and capital, no one should be fated to eat dust on the basis of their verb conjugation. Yet those are precisely the stakes in the bootstraps rhetoric so often hurled callously at the urban poor, immigrants, and those with disabilities. My swooning for beautifully rendered sentences notwithstanding, no discerning subversive would find amenable the idea of operating within a code even colloquially known as the "King's English." I'm not sure precisely who the King is, but I'm no fan of monarchies of any kind and have no interest in deploying my words in the service of extending an imperial reign. English, as far I'm concerned, is one of the most formidable weapons we have available to us in striving to topple the King. If we take Audre Lorde at her word and accept that "the master's house will never be destroyed by the master's tools," keeping the King out of our English is imperative for words to remain a vehicle for progressive change.[5]

o o o o

Reclining flat on our backs on the dusty, carpeted expanse of my living room floor, my best friend, Jonathan, and I stared in to the plaster cosmos of my apartment's crumbling ceiling. The bland, hasty paint job overhead made for a canopy of sloping, soft-serve mountains, the kind of inkblot test fodder ideal for hazy reveries on summer afternoons. Moments before, we'd chugged a container of 5-Hour Energy each, and thus began the distinct variety of petty yet hardscrabble competition we'd been engaging in since we were small enough to race each other up the playground slide. According to the rules of the game we'd invented just that morning, the first of us to successfully achieve REM sleep right there on the floor—in defiance of the potent cocktail of caffeine, energizing herbs, and god-knows-what-else galumphing insistently through his system—would be the victor. Jonathan's twenty-first birthday was a few short weeks away, and its proximity had made me reflective about the tenure of our friendship and how we'd both developed along the way. He was the first great friend I'd made when the Asims relocated to the suburbs.

"I gotta tell you, man," I blurted, surprising myself. "Don't take this the wrong way, but you've turned out, like, way smarter as an adult than I feel like your parents gave you credit for growing up."

Jonathan sat up on an elbow and opened one eye. The static charge of the carpet had raised a couple of his spirally, chestnut locks so they stood like straight-backed meerkats.

"Well, yeah," he said tolerantly. "I think back in the day they were really concerned about my learning disabilities. They're *parents*: when your kid has problems learning how to read and write early on, of course you're going to have doubts about the future."

At this, I thought about the many lengthy middle school chats we had over AOL Instant Messenger, a dated medium in which Jonathan's considerable difficulty with spelling even monosyllabic words posed a challenge. Over the years, I developed a knack for interpreting his idiosyncratic arrangement of letters and syllables, taking in his invented spellings with a familiarity almost level with the ones in my textbooks. The striking thing was that his errant constructions were clearly guided by a consistent, recognizable logic; it just didn't happen to align with the caprices of standard English.

"Dude, I still remember telling Bobby Wiley I was gonna kick the shit out of him in fifth grade if he didn't stop making fun of people in the Brown spelling group," I said, laughing. The spelling assignments were separated hierarchically at our elementary school, but they'd named the gradations after colors in the hopes of disguising which group was above grade level and which was not. Obviously this was futile, since kids have a sixth sense for ascertaining anything they can leverage to humiliate their peers. Bobby and I were in the exclusive Silver group together. He couldn't resist flaunting it and I did only slightly better at resisting strangling him.

Jonathan clenched his fist theatrically.

"He made fun of the Brown spelling group?"

"Yeah, he was a really smug overachiever prick about it."

Jonathan snorted. "But wouldn't you have been one too if you hadn't been friends with me?"

"Maybe," I admitted.

There's no doubt that having a guy like Jonathan as a running mate substantially informed my view of the world, particularly my conviction that "intelligence" didn't always manifest itself in the archetypal ways. His affable personality and phlegmatic demeanor allows him to sneak up on people, but Jonathan is a deep cat. Starting from my earliest and clumsiest forays into songwriting, he was the only one of my friends who performed accurate and expansive exegeses of all of my band's lyrics—unprompted. When I was first becoming overtly interested in politics, it was Jonathan who had hipped me to the ills of sweatshops, income inequality, and the genocide of indigenous people. If you knew him in the capacity that I did, it didn't really make sense to be too hung up on the fact that he'd probably never master the difference between "than" and "then."

"I just remember my mom always telling me to be patient with you, to not expect you to keep up with the same things I talked about with 'my egghead friends,'" I confessed. Pursuing this conversation wasn't helping me to resist the energy shot's effects, but as long as I was awake, it was in my best competitive interest to keep him up as well. "And I know that was just a reflection of your mom's neurosis about your learning disabilities—things she said to my mom when they'd have tea together or whatever."

"Totally. I can easily picture my mom saying all of that to yours."

"I mean—I feel her, I know where she was coming from. I just think it set a stunted horizon of expectation, though, hearing that all the time about you. 'Cause I mean now we're grown up, and you're one of the smartest motherfuckers I know."

"You have to realize, though. There's a reason for that."

"How do you mean?"

"With people I'm not as comfortable with, I probably don't come across as articulate as I do talking to you. With people I don't really know well, I always feel self-conscious about not speaking or reading well or whatever. I think about my disabilities more, and probably because I'm thinking about them, I stumble more."

"Self-fulfilling prophecy."

"Exactly. You probably think I seem well-spoken because when we talk one on one, I never worry about fucking up or saying the wrong thing. Even though you were always better with words, I've always felt like you speak my language."

My friendship with Jonathan, my admiration for "Stupid Little Love Song," and my nativity to unlike zones all invite me to aspire to the English of a different King. And I count my blessings, because why choose standardization when you could wrangle words with the touch and torque that LeBron James puts on an acrobatic finish in the paint?

PMA (Positivist Mental Attitude)

An Annotation of Bad Brains' "Attitude"

I had seen barbed wire before. It was sinister flora, indigenous to the place I was from, sprouting forth from the top of gangways and junkyard fences to deter the omnipresent threat of riffraff. It sneered in the sunlight as errant passes in childhood games sent whiffle balls or frisbees sailing over its head. What was novel about seeing barbed wire surrounding the building in which our uncle was now imprisoned was that I had mainly seen it used to keep people out of private property. I was in first grade, and it had never occurred to me that those gnarled, lacerating tendrils might be used to hold someone in one place.

Grandma Susie probably didn't deliberately plan on bringing me along on the trip to the outskirts of Illinois to visit her son in prison. I suspect my being left in her care and a conducive visit date just happened to intersect. After a long sojourn during which we changed city buses three or four times, we had arrived at the ambiently listless federal building and shuffled through the entry rigmarole, the rote performance of a ghetto cliché.

"What's wrong, G?" Uncle Frank asked after the squat, reticent corrections officer had fetched him. He spoke into the telephone that connected us through the glass partition separating prisoners from visitors.

"Nothing," I said tonelessly. I didn't feel glum, just overwhelmed.

"You look like something's wrong," he pressed. "Looking all serious."

It surprised me that he thought the situation called for nonchalance. *Should I look like I'm totally OK with visiting a prison?* I thought.

Maybe so.

Grandma Susie's affect throughout the visit was placid, almost businesslike. Her youngest son was condemned to a joyless hell hole at the edge of town, but she seemed to regard this with a matter-of-fact distance. At the time, her casual demeanor did not register as stoicism to my seven-year-old consciousness. I interpreted her response to her son's incarceration as evidence of the scenario's predestination: you're born, you grow up, hijinks ensue, you go to jail. This only slightly misguided takeaway is part and parcel with an extensive hidden curriculum of subaltern experience. It was reasonable to internalize a biographical forecast involving some kind of undesirable engagement with the justice system. It was not a stipulation that you needed to be a bad person in order to be eligible for this potentiality. Our uncle's own example confirmed as much.

Uncle Frank had been a lighthearted presence in my childhood. He was our mother's Favorite Sibling, the holder of a championship belt one could not say was hotly contested, as the Black Momba was generally not close with any of her siblings. But it was a meaningful designation in that he was allowed to babysit our brother Joe and me from time to time. Joe and I regarded him as a quasi-authority figure at best. He was tall, brawny, and athletic, but his supervision of us felt more like a playdate with a peer. Mostly he raided the fridge and watched cartoons while occasionally glancing into the room Joe and I shared to make certain we hadn't maimed one another. When I try to recreate Uncle Frank's symbolism in the elementary school version of my brain, I want to retroactively impose a propeller beanie at the summit of his six foot two, 250-pound do-ragged frame. It is easy to see now, of course, that my perception of him didn't translate to the larger world. While I recognized Uncle Frank as akin to the Jolly Green Giant, passersby on the street were more likely to associate him with any one of a litany of specters of robust black pathology in the cultural imagination. Ultimately, he'd lived up to the latter association on at least one occasion, and that misstep had changed his life forever.

The circumstances leading to Uncle Frank's arrest were something like this. He had impregnated a young woman who was not his girlfriend. The woman phoned Frank at some ungodly hour and asked him to go to the store—in the projects—in the middle of the night. She claimed to have called because the baby needed diapers, but it was more likely a means of keeping tabs on Frank's after-hours activities. According to the Black Momba, this was a time-honored tactic of unmarried mothers in East St. Louis. A disproportion of available men to available women in the inner-city mating pool had given rise to a feral territoriality over shared baby daddies. The Black Momba maintains that becoming ensnared in this tangled domestic situation was her brother's first mistake. On the way to the store, Frank was confronted by an irate neighbor who was high on PCP. The neighbor had challenged Frank, a decision that, in view of our uncle's physique and athletic prowess, would be surprising if it were not for the involvement of drugs. Frank tried to incapacitate the dude without killing him. But the man's PCP-enhanced resilience eventually left our mother's brother with no choice but to use deadly force. When he couldn't end the fight with his fists alone, Uncle Frank slumped the man by nailing him with a baseball bat.

The speculation favored among Mom's side of the family is that with proper legal representation Frank would have beat the rap by claiming self-defense. The man he'd killed was certainly the aggressor, and Frank had no prior convictions on his record. Factors unrelated to the details of the incident appear to have played a role in the trial's outcome, however. Our uncle relied on the services of a court-appointed attorney, and the prosecutor managed to exaggerate the tenuous link between the killing and drugs. Frank was convicted and sentenced to ten years, though he ultimately served only seven before being released early for good behavior. Of course, even once his body was no longer imprisoned, his freedom remained compromised by the stigma of having been incarcerated in the first place. Predictably, employment proved even harder to come by as a poor, black, uneducated ex-con than it had when he'd been a poor, black, uneducated ex-con-in-waiting. His criminal record even stymied efforts to cohabitate with his girlfriend—when the couple submitted applications for even the most modest housing, Frank's legal history usually disqualified them, or at least sufficiently spooked the property's owner into offering the apartment to someone else. Even after finding steady work in construction, he continued to live in Grandma Susie's house into his early forties.

I don't recall a lot more about my lone voyage to see him behind bars. Mainly I remember our mother's ire when she found out, the earful she gave Grandma Susie for exposing me to the gaping maw of the machine at such an impressionable age. She should've thanked her. That fateful visit to black America's assumed wheelhouse was clarifying in a formative way. It was a foundational clue in the coalescence of a particular vision of my place within the American story. I'd soon learn that our uncle's woes were a microcosm for the broader scenario within which African Americans find themselves in a culture congenitally disposed to destroy them. I appreciated precisely how slim the margin of error was for someone of my circumstances: a single, seemingly inconsequential choice could trigger a cascade of developments in which one does not pass go and does not collect two hundred dollars.

That early encounter with the criminal justice system deeply informed the schematic of how I operated in the world. Life, it seemed to me early on, was fairly arbitrary. "Deservingness" had no bearing on your access to resources. The system was evidently capricious and tenacious, and once the stench of reprobation marked you, essential amenities receded irretrievably despite your best efforts. If you inherited a denigrated post in the human pecking order, the difference between ascent and inertia (or shit, potentially even regression) hinged mostly on wily, vigilant overcompensation. I suppose I still believed in the American dream—within reason. I was optimistic that I could ascend from the lowly caste into which I'd been born, but only by a not purely meritocratic guerilla campaign. Sure, I felt like a free man, but one deeply in touch with the frightening and irreducible precarity of his liberty.

There was something of a counterweight to this: our young, bohemian parents were possessors of a quietly assured variant of double consciousness. They believed themselves (and by extension their children) to be members of what Fran Lebowitz would call "a natural aristocracy of talent." Mom and Baba conceded that race and class—and in our mother's case, gender—presented formidable obstacles for our family, but they believed fervently in the equalizing power of their own respective genius. It was a stance that sealed their marriage and permeated our household. The desolate expanse of blight and filth outside our doorway was a pit stop on the way to something more hallowed, even, than white picket fences and backyard tire swings: Aristotelian enlightenment. Literary adulation. Artistic fulfillment. Our folks had Joe and me in their early twenties and they parented with bounds of youthful idealism intact. We were raised to believe that systemic oppression was powerful, but our family was stronger. Mom and Baba maintained this conviction when the misfires of warring gangbangers whizzed through the kitchen window, narrowly missing Mom as she washed the dishes. They maintained this conviction when Baba walked out on his job selling television sets at Sears, resolved to make ends meet with whatever income he could generate by lassoing letters full-time. They maintained this conviction when Bumsy, the shiftless but charming Crip affiliate next door, was wheeled from his home on a stretcher, his barrel chest drenched with the namesake of the rival set who shot him.

Mom encapsulated this spirit of stubborn resilience with a pithy refrain: *Yes, the world is unjust. And? So now you know.* Her cocksure gallantry rubbed off in ways both empowering and paralyzing. It equipped me to swagger through standardized tests envisioning the achievement gap as a minotaur I could vanquish singlehandedly with the sage shading of scantron bubbles. But it was also a posturing that made me flood with shame virtually any time I succumbed to frustrated tears. Especially after the move, when my secret waterworks were often delayed responses to an endless parade of newfangled schoolyard detractors and their gleeful taunts of "faggot" and "white boy" (or when they were feeling especially creative, "faggot white boy"). Even in my more overtly rebellious teenage years, our mother's cocky credo penetrated the fog of hormones like a mantra, stabilizing me as I stumbled through the high-wire act of adolescent irreverence. Upward mobility was not merely an enterprise of guile and grit, but a sustained evasion of pitfalls and snares to which I was made especially vulnerable by virtue of my social position. As I matured, I understood it as incumbent upon me to facilitate this ascension with the same pluck that propelled Baba's ascent from talented but disadvantaged hood dweller, to debt-saddled college dropout, to someone with his own Wikipedia page.

The fulfillment of this objective, it seemed to me, demanded something less like the exploits of a traditional captain of industry than the shrewd mutiny of one of his subordinates. I imagined myself as a trespasser infiltrating a highly secure building that housed a vaunted jewel: freedom, security, health, and the realization of my ideal self. A web of interlocking, touch-sensitive lasers barricaded me from that prize. At the slightest brush of contact with this tapestry of hazards, I could be crushed by the full weight of a system designed to ensure that the jewel eluded me indefinitely. It didn't matter that I conjugated verbs, never wore sagging pants, avoided playing my music too loud, and allotted ample latitude to white pedestrians; these behaviors could only mitigate—and never fully eliminate—my vulnerability to the touch-sensitive lasers. Straight edge became attractive to me in part because it became a way of contorting and stretching between, around, and underneath the web that complicated my pursuit of the jewel. It was a way to stay nimble, loose, unencumbered, up to the gymnastic task at hand. Not drinking positioned me to avoid dependency, disinhibition, and apathy, each of which constituted a row in the gridded laser alarm system that blocked access to the jewel. Not taking drugs functionally disarmed additional strands in the tapestry of hazards, as did abstaining from reckless sexual encounters. I decided to become straight edge at fourteen, for several reasons, but none more compelling than the recognition of one, essential paradox: I could move more comfortably via the self-imposition of rigid limits.

o o o o

The same social currents that coaxed me out of the straight edge foxhole inspired Dylann Roof to kick-start a race war. The bowl cut–sporting high school dropout convicted of murdering nine people at a historic African American church in Charleston, South Carolina, named the 2012 murder of unarmed Florida teenager Trayvon Martin as a turning point in his racial politics. In his harrowing white supremacist manifesto, Roof writes that the case prompted him to "type in the words 'black on White' crime into Google, and I have never been the same since that day." Roof acknowledges having already entertained such seductively specious thoughts as "blacks were the real racists" prior to that fateful Google query, but the Martin case catalyzed a heightened consciousness in him, one upon which he felt compelled to act. I cite the parallel between Roof and me because, like many members of the millennial generation, Martin's death was transformative for me too, and nudged me toward the crystallization of some things I'd already had inklings about.

I had just turned twenty-five when I began tracking Trayvon Martin's story. I was in my sophomore year of college and living in a dorm for the first time. If it had come up in conversation, as it often did in dorm life, I'd have told you without hesitation that I was straight edge. Martin's death and the posthumous smear campaign that followed led me to seriously reconsider what straight edge meant to me for the first time. In the immediate aftermath of Martin's death, most of the press coverage hinted that Sanford police had perhaps too hastily accepted the version of events supplied by Martin's admitted killer, George Zimmerman. As the story gained steam in the national media, speculation mounted that Martin had precipitated his own death by attacking Zimmerman, that the twenty-eight-year-old neighborhood watch captain managed the mind-bending feat of being instigator, killer, and—somehow—victim. First, journalists scoured Martin's social media profiles in search of evidence to support the claim that he was a violent head case on a short, brutal path to incarceration or premature death well before his run-in with Zimmerman. Talking heads pointed to Martin's disciplinary record at school in order to caricature him as a thug, as if a suspension in tenth grade proved he must have been the aggressor in the confrontation that cost him his life. Soon

a debate raged about whether Martin's choice of attire justified his execution.

As you probably know, Gyasi, the Black Momba has long
aspired to exclude hoodies from every Asim's wardrobe. As
the mother of a black daughter and four black sons, she is a
post-doc in an accelerated version of the hidden curriculum.
For her, it is second nature to devise and implement family
policy that, at least in theory, lowers the odds of one of her
kids becoming a hashtag. She believes that Baba's longevity
and career success are made possible in part by his avoidance
of dark clothing and hooded sweatshirts.

It was a talking point in our household for as long as I
can remember: a black person's dresser drawers should be
curated to offset the benightedness suggested by their skin,
hair, lineage. I suspect that some kind of inversion of that
thinking informs the fact that hoodies and black clothes take
on hallowed significance in punk rock. Any punk band worth
its salt makes hoodies a merch table staple. By adopting punk
clothing despite the credible risks, I was doubling down on the
otherness I was urged to dilute.

Tabloid gasbag Geraldo Rivera emerged from whatever
damp crypt of C-list purgatory he'd been hiding in to advance an argument that Martin should have known better
than to wear a hoodie in a white, upscale gated community.
Respectability politics weren't new to me, of course. But it
felt like the Martin controversy unleashed the mutant strain
of it, like an extraordinarily resilient iteration of cockroach

that had evolved to withstand the perils its ancestors succumbed to. Having achieved twenty-five years in Amerikkka, I thought I'd grown blasé to the rhetorical knots into which folks contorted themselves to justify violence against black people, but, alas, such emotional remove eluded me, as it does to this day. For too many others, though, detachment was in ample supply. I was flummoxed that a significant number of adult humans could conclude that the most grievous error committed on the night Martin died was his own sartorial choice, that an extrajudicial death penalty was the fitting penance. The totemic killings that incited the Black Lives Matter movement are collective traumas that devastate once for their very happening and again in the craven, victim-blaming responses to them. Taking in so many prescriptive analyses of what kinds of behavior supposedly inoculate black people from presumed criminality, I began to consider the possible correspondence between my embrace of straight edge and the conditioning influences of black exceptionalism.

Around the same time, I'd befriended Oda, a Norwegian philosophy major who got a thrill out of pushing my ideological buttons. Because we attended a Quaker college, discussions of consent were as much a feature of our environment as invocations of the Inner Light. One of our more spirited debates was over the ramifications of rape culture. Our fundamental disagreement came down to the question of prevention. Oda believed any suggestion that a woman adjust her behavior to minimize the threat of being raped was effectively a sanctioning of rapists. For Oda, the bottom line in any conversation about the circumstances that lead to rape was that women who are raped are unequivocally blameless. It was rape apologism to even entertain the question of how best to avoid conditions that make rape more likely. I sympathized with Oda's rhetoric, but I found its practical application unworkable. Granted, as a dude I was less vulnerable to the scourge in question and was accordingly wary of making proclamations about how to handle ills that male privilege (for the most part) protected me from. Nonetheless, there were parallels I could identify with directly. I'd had to slip past the grid of touch-sensitive lasers to even set foot upon the very campus at which Oda and I had met. Should I have lunged recklessly into the tapestry of hazards on principle, just to prove their illegitimacy?

Studied self-preservation was perhaps the most essential lesson of the hidden curriculum of subaltern experience. But racial otherness and gender otherness don't always produce the same takeaways. Here, one of the telltale catchphrases in discourses on diversity is instructive: "women and people of color." Those two terms in conjunction appear to imply a mutual exclusivity that is literally false and figuratively true. It's literally false because clearly half of all racial minorities are women, and white women do constitute a political minority. It's figuratively true in that white women occupy a stratum that marks them as both dominant and marginal. White women exist in a cultural space that inclines us to on one hand asterisk their inclusion as minorities and on another to undercut their entitlement to the full benefits of whiteness.

The absence of a modifier before "women" is some evidence of this; there's a tendency to assume women are white unless specifically signaled otherwise. That position of connotative default reflects a degree of social and political centrality that reduces the extent to which they are subject to the hidden curriculum. Since Oda was a young white woman from a Scandinavian country, I figured our differences in experience influenced our divergences in moral imagination.

I think of it like this, Gyasi. If I know there's a man-eating troll under a bridge, I'm going to identify the alternate routes I could take to get to my destination without ever nearing the bridge. For me, amending my trajectory so as to never coincide with the troll does not mean I morally condone his dietary choices. It is no more than the result of the calculation that I have more control over my itinerary than his appetite for blood, and since my life depends on it, I'll opt for the more plausibly attainable change. To my mind, it is also a significant wrinkle that making this calculation does not indict the people the troll inevitably manages to catch. It's the troll's behavior that's reprehensible, but to even maintain a position from which I can condemn him, I must first remain alive.

I assumed that a similar calculus grounded African American traditions like "The Talk," the proverbial parent-child sit down in which experienced, world-weary black adults explain the sociopolitical situation of blackness to their young children. This ongoing conversation is essentially a how-to guide for navigating a world in which one is unavoidably preceded by one's four-hundred-year-old reputation. The premise of this discussion does not suppose that the four-hundred-year-old reputation is justifiable, logical, or just; the four-hundred-year-old reputation merely *is*, and, by virtue of its ontology, must be dealt with in a sustainable way. I'm not sure you were ever subject to the traditional incarnation of this chat, Gyasi. By the time you came along, self-protective black pragmatism was diffuse in the household atmosphere. It swirled in the air like asbestos in low-income housing. The Talk will often center on how to engage with police, but its import is not limited to amicable relations with our nation's finest. These lectures are also a process by which a young person is outfitted with the tools to achieve white space literacy, the ability to anticipate and perform the various concessions people of color must make in order to move safely through predominantly white environments.

My familiarity with these ideas predisposed me to take a tack opposite Oda's in our discussions of rape prevention. We agreed on the basics: any organized attempt to combat rape culture on college campuses should of course focus on discouraging the commission of rape, offering resources for students who experience sexual violence, nurturing a culture of consent, and providing students with the tools to build mutually safe, equitable relationships. Certainly the primary object of such efforts would be those who might rape rather than those who might be raped. But if I was asked to advise a given person on how to avoid rape *happening to them*, I would mention things like the buddy system and being aware of one's surroundings at night and being mindful of situations involving alcohol. I might grudgingly acknowledge that how one dresses, talks, and behaves could influence the probability of whether one becomes a target. I would not suppose that this line of thinking shifted the onus of responsibility from the potential rapist to the potential victim. I would believe I was merely delivering some variation of The Talk.

And yet . . . something about Oda's stance resonated with me. Maybe the perspective that might throw light on the way forward actually *needed* to come from someone who had not been forged in the fire of the hidden curriculum. When self-preservation is our highest aim, don't we inevitably require less from those who threaten that preservation? It was the early spring of 2012. The death of Trayvon Martin was an increasingly prominent national news item. The ill-fated seventeen-year-old was being tried in the court of public opinion for complicity in his own destruction, and the consensus view found him guilty. My back and forth with Oda coincided with my fury at the narrative developing around Martin's death. Both contributed to my increasing disenchantment with straight edge. To what extent should life be defined by capitulation to macro-level forces beyond one's control? Into what shapes might I ultimately contort myself in my eagerness to outflank the tapestry of hazards? How could I be certain that a straight edge lifestyle was anything more than a form of compensation for being black?

Having come to straight edge through the oppositional subculture of punk, I had been inclined to think of not drinking, not smoking, and not approaching sex as a conquest as a far cry from Talented Tenth moralism. But behaviorally, being edge essentially made me a paragon of Du Boisian virtue, a model of the sober, circumspect approach to living that the Bill Cosbys of the world believe can endear us to our oppressors. This seemed to me less an ideological contradiction than a problem of legibility. Moral and political choices take on varying valences depending on the context in which they occur. For instance, it's hard to imagine that the Buddha's origin story would be a narrative worth founding a religion from if he'd been a beggar who renounced earthly pleasures rather than a wealthy prince who did. If your status guarantees a wide berth, sticking to the straight and narrow recognizably constitutes a rebellion. By contrast, asceticism from a social position that is to begin with defined by deprivation is, perhaps, a tacit endorsement of the status quo. It seems like such a cruel trick. I'd wanted to emulate Minor Threat frontman Ian MacKaye, but because of personal qualities I didn't choose, I came down on the side of Newt Gingrich. A have-not who elects to have even less merely affirms the stasis of his very bereftness.

The performance of punk values or ethics is positional like anything else. The essence of punkness is the championing of the transgressive, the disruptive, the stridently antiestablishment. To be punk is to pronounce that something loftier than conventionality and sexier than societal approbation is the impetus for your style, taste, decision-making, self-concept. But the meaning of a countercultural ethos depends in large part on exactly which culture one is seeking to counter. Straight edge was an oppositional stance when it emerged in the early 1980s as a rebellion against the excesses of seventies rock star libertinism, but a decontextualized reading of its central tenets—no drugs, no drinking, no vacuous sex—could forgivably misunderstand it as a warped form of puritanism.

When Ian MacKaye sang "I'm a person just like you / But I got better things to do" in straight edge's original, titular anthem in 1981, he spoke from the vantage point of someone whose humanity was never in doubt. He reminds the listener of his personhood, his symmetry with those to whom he speaks as a means of undercutting the potential sanctimony of his message. His grasping for equality is an arm outstretched downward from an elevated perch. MacKaye does not sing from a position freighted with the legacy of subhumanity codified into law. He is a person just like you who never at any time constituted only three-fifths of one, a status that mutes the moral import of his behavioral or lifestyle choices. Asceticism performed at a credibility surplus is not congruent with the same act performed from a position of deficit.

I've mused, Gyasi, that the link between punk culture and the Black Lives Matter movement is that each is a rampart for the protection of post-conventional identity, a term I've imagined as an attempt to reconcile Cooley's looking glass self with Du Boisian double consciousness and Kohlberg's post-conventional morality. I was born with a little too much blitzkrieg bop in the blood. A vision of the self that is not self-evident is a symptom of that. But where punk and this current iteration of antiracist struggle appear to be simpatico, straight edge defies any tidy analysis of its alignment with the two.

◦ ◦ ◦ ◦

When I stumble into a conversation in which there is occasion to mention the relative paucity of African American representation in punk, several different types of people will narrow their eyes and tune out. The reasons for this can range from sentiments like (1) "OMG, black people going on about race again" to (2) "Isn't punk *supposed* to be white boy music?" to (3) "I don't have to take this—I canvassed for Obama!" But a particular kind of person purses their lips and affects a skeptical expression because they're armed with what they see as a discussion-truncating retort that they're simply waiting to uncork, so thorough and devastating in its rectitude as to render my abiding thesis moot:

"But what about Bad Brains?"

Gyasi, if you're black and known to be generally receptive to the charms of double-time drums, guttural vocals, and bruising guitar riffs, you will at some point encounter a social setting in which someone cavalierly assumes that 1989's *Quickness* is your favorite hardcore album. Doing this to someone is kind of like approaching a pale-skinned NBA aficionado and pigeonholing them as a rabid devotee of Larry Bird. For African American rockers, the legendary all-black quartet from Washington, DC, can become a bone lackadaisically tossed, a canonical yet patronizing afterthought, punk's affirmative action candidate. But Bad Brains' lasting cultural resonance cannot be dismissed. As a high school punk rocker in the suburbs of the Washington metro area, I was the enthusiastic recipient of many a CD-burning era mixtape containing manic-tempoed feral jams like "Banned in DC" and "Pay to Cum," but my primary association with Bad Brains was their endearingly platitudinal motto, PMA (positive mental attitude). Lifted from some forgotten '80s self-help book, the phrase was a catchy summary of the band's empowering outlook as articulated in their rollicking manifesto, "Attitude."

PMA formed a counterintuitive but alluring conjunction with the band's name; somehow these dudes managed to boast defective gray matter that at the same time sustained a sunny outlook. I never considered myself a pessimist per se, but my inclination was to roll my eyes at PMA as the kind of slogan that put the "bro" in bromide. Even during the early gestation of my punk rock identity, the grounded, wary sensibilities of our parents inflected my interpretation of Bad Brains' particular take on the punk ethos. I believed in myself and nurtured my faith in Dickinsonian possibility, but to do so in view of the constraints of the tapestry of hazards felt more like being an adherent of positivist mental attitude. The hidden curriculum of subaltern experience is inherently positivist; you interpret the experience of marginalization through reason and logic, and it forms the basis of authoritative knowledge when the cost of distorting or failing to absorb that knowledge is extinction. Positivist Mental Attitude accepted the existence of the grid of touch-sensitive lasers. Positivist Mental

Attitude was unpersuaded by the national mythos that touted hard work and sacrifice as panacea, that insists cream always rises no matter what. Positivist Mental Attitude encouraged the embrace of rational, scrupulous, self-sustaining practices at the expense of pacifying falsehoods.

Yes, the world is unjust. And? So now you know.

As you square off every day against the four-hundred-year-old reputation and the systems that it undergirds, my money is on you. You have great reason to bet on yourself, too. In some ways, the world is going to open up for you like forsythias in April the moment you bat those boy band eyelashes at it. But evading the tapestry of hazards long enough to build the life you deserve will take a consummate feat of fast-twitch finesse.

For much of my childhood I feared that Positivist Mental Attitude would eventually kill Baba before his time. If I'm very lucky—if the course of my life develops with even slight fidelity with my plans—Positivist Mental Attitude will certainly kill me. We are wizened by years of unmagical thinking.

I have noted with alarm the continuity between Positivist Mental Attitude and what psychologists call John Henryism, a phenomenon in which those who are disadvantaged yet preternaturally driven put nose to grindstone with such intensity as to functionally work themselves to death. Writing for *The Atlantic*, James Hamblin makes the case that while self-control is an asset for overcoming challenging backgrounds, the level of restraint that makes upward mobility possible can have a profoundly debilitating impact on physical health.

"Even in the worst circumstances, people with the most self-control and resilience have the highest likelihood of defying odds—poverty, bad schools, unsafe communities—and going on to achieve much academically and professionally," he writes. "Except that even when that is possible, those children seem to age rapidly in the process. That is, their cells *visibly age before their time* among other undesirable effects on the body, according to research published this week from Northwestern University and the University of Georgia."[1]

That's not to say that self-control and resilience are innately self-destructive traits. The context in which high self-regulation occurs determines whether degenerative effects are concomitant. "The exact opposite correlation exists in advantaged kids: Self-control is associated with all sorts of positive health outcomes," Hamblin observes. "Only in the disadvantaged communities does this paradox exist: good outcomes on the behavioral/educational/psychosocial side, but apparently at a cost to physical health."

Just as the efficacy of principled asceticism as social dissent is positional, so too are its biological repercussions. Keeping one's self on a short leash as a have is a boon. Doing so as a have-not is an incremental tightening of one's own noose. There are a number of theories as to why this is, Hamblin writes:

> One is that it's the climb up the ladder that takes the toll. . . .
> When you come from disadvantaged class/race/place, you
> have greater obstacles to overcome. You're likely in schools

that are underfunded and understaffed. You come from a small town that had fewer resources and opportunities, and your parents were struggling in challenging economic conditions. You don't have the tutors and after-school resources that affluent suburban kids do. So to get to the same place—say, to graduate from college—takes a lot more energy and bandwidth.

It's striking that signs of accelerated physical aging tend to coincide with the adoption of a mature-beyond-one's-years lifestyle. So much of the romance surrounding recreational substance use centers on the transience of youth, the urgency of seizing the fleeting interval during which possibilities are many and consequences are few. This is probably why being straight edge so often arouses reflexive disdain: a life purposefully devoid of substances and casual sex registers to some as an untimely descent into voluntary geriatrics. Positivist Mental Attitude can necessitate such a plunge. Neither of our parents had the kind of blearily experimental, hallucinogenic adolescence or early adulthood that I grew up watching my friends experience from a distance. "Straight edge" wasn't a term in Mom's or Baba's vernacular, but there was no room for drugs or alcohol in the disciplined, conscientious habits they'd each cultivated as teenagers with plans to flee inner-city dystopias. When our mother met our father on the Reagan-era campus of Northwestern University, they were both juggling multiple part-time jobs along with a full load of courses, and struggling to feed themselves on Sundays, when the campus dining hall was customarily closed. Positivist Mental Attitude got them to that world, and if these findings are to be believed, was just as quickly pushing them out.

o o o o

The studies that Hamblin compiles point to a reality in which premature aging in its figurative sense unhappily overlaps with age's literal manifestations. It's a classic bait and switch. The most pragmatic blueprint for studied self-preservation can grease the wheels for summary annihilation. ATTN Gwendolyn Brooks: apparently you needn't lurk late, strike straight, sing sin, or thin gin in order to die soon.[2]

Whatever People Say I Am, That's What Omnaut

An Annotation of Masked Intruder's
"Take What I Want"

"You'll never be rich. You know why? Because you're afraid to go to jail."

The way Baba tells it, our great-grandfather believed that the above dictum summed up the predicament of any promising African American living in the United States. According to Baba, our great-grandfather Ed perceived himself as the smartest, most capable person he knew.

"If I wasn't a colored man, I'd be president of the United States," he used to drawl earnestly in his Mississippi twang.

Born to sharecroppers and without any formal education, Ed believed that if America was a true meritocracy, he would ascend to the highest echelons of economic prosperity and political power on the strength of his God-given genius alone. But in recognition of the social and historical barriers to his success, Ed reasoned that his genius could only propel him about half that distance—and that it would have to do so via criminal means. By the time I was born, our great-grandfather was a reticent, kindly old dude with a distinct aura of authoritative grace, but it didn't take a whole lot of eavesdropping to pick up on the stories of his extraordinary exploits as an infamous St. Louis crime lord. One anecdote that Ed's daughter, our paternal grandmother, Joyce, liked to tell stands out.

When Grandma Joyce was a teenager, an older man who was a local boxer tried to take her home from a party. Knowing that no one at the party could challenge him physically, the man swaggered up to our grandmother and demanded her hand despite having never encountered her before. Our grandma's brother, Thraceton, had accompanied her to the gathering. He politely but firmly told the man that Joyce would not be going home with him. Later that week, Grandma's would-be suitor turned up at Thraceton's high school and waited for the much younger Thraceton to walk home. The boxer intercepted Thraceton and savagely beat him to a pulp in retribution for having come between him and the girl he'd set his sights on. When our great-grandfather Ed saw his oldest son walk through the door severely battered and bruised, he had already begun formulating a plot for vengeance. After Thraceton explained what had happened, our great-grandfather rallied his sidekick, Lou, a laconic bruiser who flanked Ed everywhere he went in public. The duo found the boxer who had thrashed Thraceton and, according to

Grandma Joyce's straight-faced testimony, killed the man before depositing his body in the Mississippi River under the cover of darkness that very night.

Our great-grandfather Ed handled all of his affairs with that same brutal efficiency and any-means-necessary ethos. Ed took our father's brother, Uncle D, under his wing and made him the fence for Ed's merchandizing of stolen goods. Uncle D's house in North St. Louis was filled with hot items, and when a group of thieves figured out where our great-grandfather hid his considerable stash, local St. Louis news stations broadcast the ensuing raid live on the six o'clock news. Undeterred by the setback and never one to leave a family member high and dry, Ed paid off a coterie of local city officials so that Uncle D avoided even a moment of hard time. Ed continued the operation in the wake of the raid, moving his storehouse to a new, more secure location.

In first grade, when I was assigned a project on family history, I'd proudly related the tale of how my great-granddaddy Ed opened the first ever black-owned taxicab company in all of Missouri. The story moved me in part because I saw myself as an heir to the determination and rugged intelligence that enabled Ed to circumvent both his humble beginnings and the virulent racism that was endemic to his day. When I finished the presentation, my predominantly white classmates at the esteemed lefty private school I attended clapped and grinned broadly. They were already being indoctrinated with the tall tale that hard work and discipline can surmount any structural inequity. I knowingly left out the part about Gateway Cabs being a front for Ed's gambling, money laundering, and burglary schemes.

It's no accident that Uncle D—and not our father—was groomed as Ed's operative. Even when they were middle school kids, D's ripeness for the task was as obvious as Baba's unfitness; while our uncle spent his summers shadowing his grandfather and making money gassing and servicing Ed's taxis, Baba was away living on the local state university campus and taking accelerated math courses. But despite never becoming Ed's direct acolyte, Baba clearly shared qualities with Ed that his brother did not. Readily identifiable as a Talented Tenth member from as early as fourth grade, Baba was pulled from his local elementary school and placed in a gifted and talented program across town from fifth grade onward. The same year, Uncle D, who was two years Baba's senior, was relocated from a mainstream junior high to a remedial school. It would be easy to draw a genetic line connecting our father's intellectual promise and the aptitude Ed prided himself on having. But unlike Ed, Baba's gifts were validated from an early age. He was accordingly coaxed toward the straight and narrow and encouraged to believe that he could escape poverty by legal means. At the same time, by way of Ed's influence and his own burgeoning awareness of the world, Baba grew up with the understanding that the avenues to success wouldn't roll out red carpets for him just because he was talented and motivated. He was still black, still poor, and it was still the early 1970s.

The disconnect between our father's sense of morality and Ed's became glaringly apparent by the time Baba reached college. Having developed a casual interest in photography while at Northwestern, Baba phoned Ed to ask him for a camera. Ed agreed right away and promised to send him one. When the package arrived a few days later, Baba was enthused to find that the camera was a top-dollar, state-of-the-art contraption better suited for a veteran photographer than a collegiate dilettante.

"Thanks for the camera, granddaddy," our father breathed into the phone. "It's great. Where'd you get it?"

Ed chuckled for a moment.

"Off somebody's neck," he boasted.

That my great-grandfather might jack some poor sap for his expensive camera when he wasn't looking was completely consistent with everything my father knew about Ed. Though he didn't ask for details, Baba pictured Lou overtaking a hapless photo geek from behind and snatching the goods from his shoulders like a jungle cat picking off an unwitting gazelle from the watering hole. Baba realized then that even consulting Ed as a resource was freighted with a moral weight that our father saw as an albatross. Baba was mortified at the thought that his instant gratification could come at the direct expense of another's misfortune.

"It really bothered me that someone had very possibly had to work their ass off for that camera," Baba has said.

My perception of my own sociopolitical situation was informed by both of these men's examples, but I've never had the stomach for the unseemly activities that Ed viewed as his only recourse in a society that underestimated him profoundly. If my two forebears represent opposite poles of approaches to negotiating marginalization, then I certainly fall nearer to our father, who went on to become an author, journalist, and writing professor. I don't meet our great-grandfather's precondition for becoming rich. Avoiding prison is something like my second- or third-highest priority in life. But I am also realistic enough to know that his assessment of the terrain for promising black Americans is far from obsolete, even though the first time I was old enough to cast a vote for the presidency I did so for a man with the same complexion as Ed.

During my first year of college, Cornel West came to campus to deliver an address on Manning Marable, the late writer and Columbia professor most famous for a biography of Malcolm X that earned him a Pulitzer Prize for history. West noted that prior to becoming a world-famous orator and civil rights leader, Malcolm was a petty hustler named Detroit Red who ended up in prison because of his "gangster proclivities." I felt Ed's spirit had to be in the room when West went on to say that the young Malcolm's gangster proclivities were not a product of shaky scruples but of an appreciation for the magnitude of the powers at work in American life that conspired to destroy him. One could not criticize Malcolm's unsavory past without what West called giving him "a dialectical reading." West suggested that any discerning black person aware of themselves as a colonial subject would grapple with gangster proclivities. He acknowledged that it was an intractable source of tension within himself. As West saw it, Malcolm ended up in jail because he'd opted for taking arms against a sea of troubles, which was the same reasoning that led Ed down a criminal path of his own. West, Malcolm, and my great-grandfather each concluded that suffering the slings and arrows of outrageous fortune is an ignoble, losing proposition. The difference between survival and annihilation, then, was not a matter of whether one harbors gangster proclivities but whether one could channel such irreverence in a fashion that filled lecture halls rather than jail cells.

When West didn't stop there, Ed must've gone from rolling over in his grave to pop-locking in it. The luxuriantly coiffed "democratic intellectual" pointed out that the same personal qualities that made Malcolm's youth criminal could've made a comparable white man presidential. At this, I thought of West Indian Archie, the prodigious numbers-runner in *The Autobiography of Malcolm X* who performs complex calculations in his head to swindle gamblers. If Archie had been born in a different time or to a family of superior means, he likely could have become a CEO of a multinational corporation. If he'd been positioned to leverage the same cunning and ferocity to exploit shareholders rather than drug dealers, couldn't he be someone who profits off of prisons instead of someone in and out of them? The same thing we decry as deviance in one man we laud as courage, fortitude, and ingenuity in another. Circumstances often trump individual agency in dictating whether one is canonized as a captain of industry or censured as a robber baron.

In a way, West was articulating a perspective that had already been germinating within me ever since I was old enough to talk, but as a child of integration I couldn't help my reflexive wariness at even subtle glamorization of the term "gangster." Gangsters, in the post-NWA sense of the word, are the dominant and often imaginary avatars of black dysfunction. Few archetypes in history have done more to demean the striving of the urban poor than the images of loud, lewd, and lawless men in sagging pants, lurking in the nightmares of Sean Hannity devotees everywhere. But any description of gangster roles in the cultural imagination that excludes their scintillating appeal as pop musicians is incomplete. The slang and couture of caricaturized ghetto desperadoes have been among the most propulsive forces in hip-hop's meteoric rise. Of course, even as the gangster aesthetic has been monetized, co-opted, and endlessly reproduced, the trope remains an omnipresent bogeyman used to police Talented Tenth types from doing things to undermine their progress narratives.

Don't wear a hooded sweatshirt at night because you might be confused for—*gasp*—a gangster!

Don't wear your cap backward in public because that's what gangsters do!

Only gangsters drive around the neighborhood with their stereos turned up too loud!

As a younger man, I sneered at figures like Tupac Shakur, an emcee who had insisted on referring to himself as a thug even after he became a wealthy international celebrity, because he "came from the gutter" but was "still here."[1] The idea that someone in Shakur's situation could continue to relate to those still confined to inner city foxholes seemed like a laughable overreach for authenticity. But I also feared that Shakur's visibility as a symbol of menace made it more difficult for Joe to walk home from work without arousing police suspicion. Surely there was a level of presumed criminality that Shakur and other young black people were already contending with in social spaces; did he really have to compound matters by openly embracing thuggery as a philosophy? Looking back, it was probably this trepidation about how gangster proclivities filtered through the white gaze that precluded my realizing the link between our great-grandfather's ethos and Tupac's. It felt contrary to P*MA to assume a mantle that marks you as an internal enemy of civil society openly and in bold print.

It was later still that I acknowledged the overlap between gangsta posturing and punk rock attitude and how the recognition of one's subaltern status enhances the magnetic pull of both comportments. Masked Intruder, a four-piece melodic punk band in the tradition of Screeching Weasel or Mr. T Experience, stands at the nexus of those gangsta and punk logics. Over the course of their career, they've maintained an unwavering commitment to the outlaw gimmick, to which their band name alludes. The lyrics all relate to crime, incarceration, or lovelorn behavior that leads to each. Each member performs in a different colored mask to conceal their identities, and the respective colors of their masks serve as their code names. At live shows, a "court appointed" cop named Officer Bradford acts as a satirical hype man. In most of punk culture, only Nazi punks sport a lower approval rating than police. Somehow though, in Masked Intruder's universe, the arm of the state forgoes its typical chokehold to instead reach out to slap you a sweaty high five. Partially because the members are all white men and partially because they sing chipper, three-chord ditties peppered with na na nas, their aestheticization of theft, stalking, and aggravated battery is generally received by their audience as more kitschy than threatening. The final track on your mixtape, Masked Intruder's "Take What I Want," is about the joys of casual burglary and the absence of remorse. The song's rootsy guitar work and blue-eyed soul vocal melody are a slight departure from Masked Intruder's usual formula, which mostly resembles the Ramones but with higher production value and campy doo-wop vocal arrangements. "Take What I Want" rocks like if Angus Young was raised on a steady diet of New Found Glory.

I imagine that our great-grandfather might appreciate "Take What I Want" on a literal level, but it also speaks to the freewheeling approach I've used to engage with counterculture. I've always taken what I wanted from books and music regardless of whether I belonged to the demographic at which it was aimed. Doing so has been as much a matter of survival as actual criminal activity might have been for Ed. Ed and I are united in distinct but related forms of defiance, both of which stem from the vivid awareness that convention is by design inimical to our interests. Ed's rebellion broke laws while mine mainly confounds the de facto riders affixed to them. Insofar as I am ever guilty of "acting like a white boy," I aspire to and occasionally do engage with the world with the same jubilant abandon as a Masked Intruder song. Is there a purer expression of freedom surfeit than using imagined persecution as a party trick?

Masked Intruder's entire shtick is an elaborate cosplay of the danger that you and I court by being. Indeed, we're susceptible to being received as masked intruders even when we're undisguised and actively being intruded upon. Such was the fate of Ahmaud Arbery, a twenty-five-year-old black man stalked, shot, and killed by a former police officer and his son in late February 2020. There are eerie parallels between the killing of Arbery and the loss of Trayvon Martin eight years earlier. Both Arbery and Martin were executed by white vigilantes who claimed to misidentify each young man as a burglary suspect. Martin's killer, George Zimmerman, believed that Martin was casing houses. Arbery's killers, Gregory McMichael and Travis McMichael, said that their victim resembled a thief they claimed to have previously recorded on a surveillance camera.

If Zimmerman's explanation seemed doubtful, unbecoming synecdoche supplied a crude and wrongheaded alibi. Shortly after Martin's killing became national news, a chain email began circulating that alleged that a photo of the six-four, thirty-one-year-old, heavily tattooed Jayceon Terrell Taylor, known by the stage name The Game, was what Trayvon actually looked like at the time of his death.[2] The confusion is revealing. The Game sells records by stylizing the attributes that Martin was presumed to have and was killed for supposedly having. When Arbery's story broke, the similarities with Martin's revived a thought experiment on social media that was most memorably posted on a video blog from actress Amandla Stenberg's Tumblr, in which she wonders, "What would America be like if we loved black people as much as we love black culture?"[3]

So-called love for the culture and apparent disdain for the people have a mutually constitutive relationship. The black culture that this collective "we" loves does not for the most part provide antibodies for the pestilence that is antiblackness. Rather, it is very often the case that the most widely beloved black culture hosts pathogens that sustain antiblackness. In a society where capitalism intonates all things, it can be easy to forget that what is commodified isn't always valued. Resolving the dissonance between the love for black culture and the antipathy for its authors would not be a matter of merely extending the love of black culture so that it also includes those who produce it. In fact, seeing black people as cherished members of the human family might meaningfully diminish the mass appeal of the art we create. Black culture that is embraced by a nonblack audience usually provides an inviting portal through which to be safely titillated by what would otherwise terrify. For some readers, Gyasi, even this book, this mixtape, and the conversation I am having with you through it will plug neatly into that equation.

What we call nonblack people's "love" for black culture is often more like the zeal visitors feel for the lions' habitat at the zoo. We would not expect that enthusiasm to carry over to encounters with lions in hospitals, in voting booths, in classrooms, in gated communities. To recognize us not as fearsome beasts but as human peers would legitimize our presence in the latter zones, but it would sure take the fun out of zoo access.

These kinds of cultural riddles were exactly what I hoped to explore the semester that I cautiously enrolled in Intro to Sociology at a local community college. My sociology professor there reminded me of the kind of person who loiters at a local gym and casually alludes to a career as a professional athlete in a past life. She had gotten her PhD at Yale, so even though she was now teaching at a community college, she wanted all the students in her charge to know she was slumming it a bit. She could easily take her talents elsewhere. We were so blessed to be under the tutelage of someone with an Ivy League pedigree for a fraction of the cost. It was admittedly somewhat grating, but I had patience for the professor's relentless chest-thumping because I thought I understood where it was coming from. She was a black woman intellectual after all. I assumed that constantly touting her credentials was a reflex she developed in response to having her considerable skills and know-how questioned or dismissed at every turn.

I was twenty and living in a shabby apartment across the street from the community college campus, playing in Some Like It Hot, and slinging Americanized Chinese food to pay the rent. Attending her class on Tuesdays and Thursdays was a relished intermission from serfdom. To some degree, I recognized I was not quite punching in the appropriate weight class myself; I had no track record of success as a student, but it was clear to me that the level of curiosity and investment I brought to the class was unusual for the setting. It's difficult to describe my predicament at the time without sounding elitist. I don't mean to hierarchize interests or pastimes. In choosing to focus on rock 'n' roll at the direct expense of four-year college, I had constructed an environment for myself that neglected a core need. At this time, my social world was something like the intellectual equivalent of a food desert. The resources I would need to put together a balanced cognitive breakfast, so to speak, were surpassingly hard to come by. Neither the clubs Some Like It Hot played in, nor the elaborate parties that my restaurant compatriots organized after work, nor the suburban hangout spots I frequented on weekends were hubs of incisive conversation.

So it's possible that in class I behaved like a ravenous person set loose at a sumptuous buffet. Some class sessions would devolve into vigorous but respectful volleys between the instructor and me. Needless to say, I didn't make any new friends this way, but gained something perhaps more valuable—affirmation that I could belong and even thrive in a scholastic setting.

At the conclusion of the class, the professor pulled me aside.

"Where are you from, young man?" she asked.

This question is, in social justice circles, at this point a punchline. What does one who asks it actually want to find out? Is the objective to learn your heritage, or your economic background? Would she be satisfied if I told her what neighborhood I went to high school in, or does she need to know where I have passports? Does anyone ask the question innocently, or does it always reflect some niggling need to taxonomize, to square someone's appearance with the category that would best explain the person? I knew that because the professor was from West Africa, there was a possibility that she did not feel the same warm and easy affinity for me that she might if she was from West Baltimore. The community college was in a suburb of DC, where blackness as a racial group came in many variants, and solidarity often hinged on likeness across axes of race and nationality together more than color alone. Nonetheless, if my instructor had been white, I would have been more suspicious. I would have taken her phrasing as code for, "to what aberrant circumstances do we owe the existence of a seemingly affable, well-spoken black boy?"

Despite her best efforts to be neutral, some of the professor's politics had already shone through in her presentation of the course material. She seemed reasonable enough. So I told her I'd grown up in a suburb on the other side of the pike, and before that I'd lived in an urban area in the Midwest, which was where my family was from.

"But where are you and your family *really* from?" She pressed, raising an eyebrow. "You've been my best student, so I know you can't be African American."

The confidence blew my hair back a bit. She was startlingly certain of the mutual exclusivity of "best student" and

"African American," so convinced that the story she told herself to survive was airtight. I can't remember precisely what my reply was. I know that I set the record straight about my origins and made clear that I registered the comment as a profound insult. I mentioned that this was a dispiriting confirmation of something I suspected anyway—namely that some black people who were fewer generations removed from the motherland giddily signed on to the consensual American hallucinations about slave-descended black folks. What I didn't process until later was how much it stung that a woman who taught a discipline intended to probe social context based on reasons and evidence was so dearly committed to a stereotype. When it came to placing me, all her vaunted Yale training went out of the window.

Needless to say, our relationship ended on a sour note. I wasn't going to be able to reach out to her for a letter of recommendation when it came time to transfer to a four-year college. If earning an A in the class meant I had finally landed a fingertip or two on a rung that had until then been just out of reach, immediately alienating the teacher certainly loosened that already tenuous grip.

It was a setback that might feel crushing, save for the fact that by twenty years old I was well practiced in punk rock attitude and in post-conventional identity. When Some Like It Hot's momentum stalled, I would go on taking community college classes piecemeal until I earned enough credits to transfer elsewhere. I set upon a winding journey to two degrees and eventually became a professor myself. All of which required acting in accord with a vision of myself that was explicitly spoken *out of* existence. I don't think this outcome can be merely accredited to resilience or the bullish tugging of bootstraps. In having learned to sit serenely in the ordinary simultaneity of best studenthood and African Americaness, I believe I am walking in Ed's footsteps. That legacy of rugged improvisation, of taking what you want belongs to you, too. It might not scan as a robust tradition to those who are not heir to it.

This came to a head when a close relative of ours was expecting her second child. The relative and I were standing in the living room of the apartment that she, her one-year-old daughter, and I shared. The family member and I were discussing possible names for the next-generation Asim who was still in utero. I suggested the name Amandla, which a cursory search through a book of African American baby names had revealed was a Xhosa word for "power." A Nelson Mandela biopic had just come to theaters, and I had been touched by the scenes in which the South African revolutionary fired up his supporters by shouting "Amandla!" (Power!) and the crowd cried back "Ngawethu!" (It is ours!)

Our relative didn't veto the suggestion outright. But she was hesitant because the name was not Ivorian. Born in Paris to immigrants from Ivory Coast, she'd immigrated to the US as a young child. Her Ivorian lineage was a source of pride, and she wanted to choose a name for her child that reflected her child's history. Of course, the new arrival would inherit history from our side of the family as well. I reminded the

married-in family member that my own surname was Swa-
hili and Arabic. Baba and the Black Momba had chosen Asim
when they changed their names in college, I explained. It
meant "protector" and suited us just fine. None of our known
ancestors spoke either of the languages our name came from,
but identity markers of our own devising were a family touchstone, a means by which we reclaimed power taken from us.

"Well, that's different," our relative protested, "because I
actually *have a culture*."

Italics definitely hers, bruh. Therein lies why I have
stumped so hard for beginning and maintaining a lifelong
project of enlightened self-invention—because for you and I
and countless others like us, the alternative is a social and political nullity worse than death.

I smiled to myself when I noticed the screen name you
chose when you joined Twitter. You told me you came up
with your handle—Omnaut—by combining two roots you'd
picked up in Latin class: "omni" meaning "all" and "naut"
meaning "voyager." I cracked that this was an odd sobriquet
for someone who rarely left the house, but I understood. I
know you to be an intrepid thinker willing to plumb great
depths and mine broad sources, including those not designed
with you in mind. The choice of Omnaut struck me as a
modern realization of an old Henry James quote: "Try to be
one of the people on whom nothing is lost." Any good mixtape is indebted to this ethic of discerning but miscellaneous
accumulation. We rely upon the same as we build and are

always refurbishing a post-conventional self. The hallmark of a life lived well, according to Whitman, is that the flesh should become a great poem. Its contents should become a dope mixtape.

Riffing on the racial aphasia at your high school, you observed recently that there's a pervasive American tendency to attach all Asian people to China and all Latinx folks to Mexico. Regardless of their actual national origin, a person who appears to be Latinx is often referred to as Mexican and an East Asian–looking person is eventually called Chinese. You asked what the equivalent misnomer might be for African Americans. The imperfect analogy I drew pointed to black folks and "the ghetto." Not the ghetto as it might be understood through personal experience or even clinical observation, but the ghetto as it exists in popular consciousness. The ghetto is presumed to be the cradle of black civilization, the point of departure for all of blackness, the standard that all black behavior, thinking, and lifestyles must be judged against. Trying to live as if your most essential self proceeds from this unstable nucleus is flatly radioactive.

In Ben Lerner's essay "Contest of Words," he suggests that suburban white boys mimic the speech and appropriate the symbols of black gangsta culture because white suburbia offers no cultural grounding for establishing more sincere identities.[4] Using black culture as a foil to understand the tics of sagging, ciphering, crip walking white boys, he allows that the behavior such white boys are copying is "exaggerated."

Lerner leaves unexamined the question of whether the behavior is itself honest, as if blackness innately provides a gritty
and enviable authenticity. We may not have generational
wealth or equal protection under the law, but dagnabit we
always have that feral realness to fall back on. When I watch
Harlem teenagers skulking the streets in skinny jeans and Jordan sneakers, I wonder how many of them feel "authentic"
or that their choices of clothing, language, and hobbies are
theirs alone, unburdened from social pressure.

Me? I can only testify to the merits of choosing to locate
the crux of blackness where gangster proclivities and punk
rock attitude meet. In 2008, *Rolling Stone* asked Cornel West
what he'd say to those who doubted whether a presidential
candidate named Barack Obama was black enough. His reply foreshadowed his eventual disenchantment with Obama,
as Obama's policy making would ultimately fall short of the
blackness standard that West laid out:

> What black people were talking about when they ques-
> tioned his blackness were the ways that, for instance, Thur-
> good Marshall was black and Clarence Thomas isn't. For
> black people, Jesse Jackson is black enough and Alan Keyes
> is not. That is, they wondered whether Obama was bold
> enough to talk about justice, to put truth to power, to side
> with the weak against the strong. That's what blackness
> means to most black people. It doesn't have anything to
> do with family lineage. It has everything to do with whom
> they side with.[5]

This definition of what it means to be black could just as well be a definition of what it means to be punk: to embrace an oppositional relationship to dominant power, to brandish skepticism as strength and a source of life-progressing momentum. West thought we were getting a punk president, and he was disgusted to find that we ended up with a poser.

○ ○ ○ ○

For you and me, siding with the weak against the strong so happens to be a matter of family lineage. And whatever you make of all this, you can count on me to side with you, until the day they lean my Operation Ivy snapback jauntily atop my headstone. Give this a few spins and let me know what you think. I'll see ya in the pit.

Acknowledgments

This book and its author are indebted to the support, guidance, and wisdom of my parents, Liana and Jabari Asim; my grandparents, Susie Ward, James and Joyce Smith; my siblings, Joe, Indigo, Jelani, and Gyasi; my mentors, Dr. Sylvia Spears, Professor Margo Jefferson, Professor Wendy S. Walters, and Professor Leslie Jamison; my colleagues, Professor Kimberlé Crenshaw and Professor Luke Charles Harris and everyone at the AAPF; and my bandmates, Rhiana Hernandez and Jake Lazaroff.

I would like to thank my visionary agent, Edward Maxwell, and canny editor, Maya Fernandez, for their belief in this project and their patient attention to seeing the book to fruition. Special thanks to Rakia Clark for getting the party started.

Thanks to Sasha Bonét, Mary Wang, Sabrina Alli, and Carina del Valle Schorske for your readership, inspiration, generative conversation, and camaraderie.

Props also to Jonathan Wiens and family, Chris Craver, Lance Giles, Carlton Norris Mabrey, Madeline Cameron

Wardleworth and family, Aziza Tichavakunda, Andrew Weiss, Patrick Cronin and family, Jihan Shaarawi, Thomas Ordaya, Kristin Damo, Maya Cooper, Paula Penn-Nabrit, Dara Malina, Mary Morris, Kevin N. Keegan, and Orla Tinsley, all of whom are integral to this book's existence.

Up the punx.

Notes

AFRICA HAS NO HISTORY

1. Henry Louis Gates Jr., *The Henry Louis Gates, Jr. Reader*, ed. Abby Wolf (New York: Basic Civitas Books, 2012), 428–29.

2. Hugh Trevor-Roper, *The Past and the Present: History and Sociology*, no. 42 (February 1969): 3–17.

3. Albert Murray, *Collected Essays and Memoirs* (New York: Library of America, 2016).

4. Justin Wolfers, David Leonhardt, and Kevin Quealy, "1.5 Million Missing Black Men," *New York Times*, April 20, 2015, https://www.nytimes.com/interactive/2015/04/20/upshot/missing-black-men.html.

5. Jonathan Lethem, "My Disappointment Critic," *Los Angeles Review of Books*, November 2011, https://lareviewofbooks.org/article/my-disappointment-critic.

6. Maria Popova, "The Art of 'Negative Capability': Keats on Embracing Uncertainty and Celebrating the Mysterious," *Brain Pickings*, November 1, 2012, https://www.brainpickings.org/2012/11/01/john-keats-on-negative-capability.

7. Christopher Sorrentino, "Success and Freedom," http://www.christophersorrentino.com/success-and-freedom.html, accessed May 12, 2020.

8. Chimamanda Ngozi Adichie, "The Dangers of a Single Story," YouTube video, 18:34, October 7, 2009, https://youtu.be/D9Ihs241zeg.

9. Wesley Morris, "In Movies and on TV, Racism Made Plain," *New York Times*, August 23, 2017, https://www.nytimes.com/2017/08/23/arts/television/white-hot-supremacist-summer.html.

10. Jay-Z, "Moonlight," YouTube video, 8:38, August 11, 2017, https://www.youtube.com/watch?v=FCSh48OlvMo.

11. Elizabeth Chin, "Ethnically Correct Dolls: Toying with the Race Industry," *American Anthropologist* 101, no. 2 (June 1999): 305–19.

12. Louis Menand, "Young Saul: The Subject of Bellow's Fiction," *New Yorker*, May 4, 2015, https://www.newyorker.com/magazine/2015/05/11/young-saul.

13. Katy Waldman, "The Tolstoy of the Zulus, The Citizen Kane of Video Games. Subsumptive Analogies are the Hitler of Figurative Speech!," *Slate*, September 17, 2015, https://slate.com/human-interest/2015/09/subsumptive-analogies-unless-you-write-ad-copy-stick-to-regular-similes-instead.html.

14. "Issa Rae of 'Insecure' Pitches a '90210' for Black Kids," YouTube video, 1:33, posted by the *New Yorker*, August 28, 2017, https://youtu.be/viZ378W15sQ.

15. Waldman, "The Tolstoy of the Zulus."

16. Danuta Kean, "Bigmouth Strikes Again: Row over Morrissey's James Baldwin Tour T-Shirt," *Guardian*, March 20, 2017, https://www.theguardian.com/books/2017/mar/20/bigmouth-strikes-again-row-morrissey-james-baldwin-t-shirt-the-smiths.

EVIDENCE OF THINGS UNSCENE

1. Eugene Holley, "What Albert Murray Taught Us About Jazz," October 19, 2020, https://www.npr.org/sections/ablogsupreme/2013/08/24/214831904/what-albert-murray-taught-us-about-jazz.

2. Charles Bukowski, "Style," Genius, https://genius.com/Charles-bukowski-style-annotated, accessed October 19, 2020.

3. Carrie Stetler, "Junot Diaz: Man in the Mirror," NJ.com, updated April 1, 2019, https://www.nj.com/entertainment/arts/2009/10/junot_diaz_man_in_the_mirror.html.

4. Seth Shostak, "Fermi Paradox," SETI Institute, April 19, 2018, https://www.seti.org/seti-institute/project/fermi-paradox.

5. The Miscreant, "Aye Nako: An Interview with the Miscreant," April 12, 2015, https://issuu.com/themiscreant/docs/the_miscreant_-_issue_58.

MARCHING THROUGH THE MOSH PIT

1. Bree Newsome, "The Civil-Rights Movement's Generation Gap," *Atlantic*, King issue, https://www.theatlantic.com/magazine/archive/2018/02/bree-newsome-generation-gap/552554, accessed September 2, 2020.

MAD PROPS TO MADNESS

1. Langston Hughes, "Suicide's Note," Poetry Foundation, https://www.poetryfoundation.org/poems/147906/suicide39s-note, accessed September 13, 2020.

2. ABC News, "Elliot Rodger: Inside the Mind of a Killer," YouTube video, 8:11, May 28, 2014, https://youtu.be/QJc234jkJ2w.

3. Jack Kerouac, *The Dharma Bums* (New York: Penguin Classics, 2006).

4. David Astramskas, "1995 Pizza Hut Commercial with Spurs' David Robinson and Dennis Rodman," *Ballislife* (blog), November 9, 2014, https://ballislife.com/1995-pizza-hut-commercial-with-spurs-david-robinson-and-dennis-rodman.

5. Jack Kerouac, *Pomes All Sizes: Pocket Poets Number 48* (San Francisco: City Lights Books, 1992), 158.

EVER SINCE I WAS A LITTLE GRRRL

1. *The Wire*, "Cleaning Up," Amazon Prime Video, 56:16, September 2, 2002, https://www.amazon.com/gp/video/detail/B003AYJ6FS/ref=atv_dl_rdr?autoplay=1.

2. Mallory Yu, "*I Am Not Your Negro* Gives James Baldwin's Words New Relevance," NPR, February 3, 2017, https://www.npr.org/2017/02/03/513311359/i-am-not-your-negro-gives-james-baldwins-words-new-relevance.

3. "The Combahee River Collective Statement," BlackPast, https://www.blackpast.org/african-american-history/combahee-river-collective-statement-1977, accessed September 13, 2020.

TO THE EDGE AND BACK

1. Tim McMahan, "The Explosion: Defining Punk in the '00s," *Lazy-I*, November 27, 2002, http://www.timmcmahan.com/explode .htm.

2. Leon Hurley, "Chekhov's Gun Is the Movie Trope That'll Ruin Everything Once You Know About It," *GamesRadar*, February 1, 2017, https://www.gamesradar.com/chekhovs-gun-the-movie-trope-thatll -ruin-everything-once-you-know-about-it.

3. Noah Yoo, "Two Alleged Victims of Brand New's Jesse Lacey Detail Years of Sexual Exploitation of Minors," *Pitchfork*, November 13, 2017, https://pitchfork.com/news/two-alleged-victims-of-brand -news-jesse-lacey-detail-years-of-sexual-exploitation-of-minors.

4. Mary Papenfuss, "Surgeon General Singles Out People of Color to Stop Alcohol, Drugs in Covid-19 Fight," *Huffington Post*, April 10, 2020, https://www.huffpost.com/entry/surgeon-general-jerome -adams-minorities-drugs-drinking-tobacco-covid-19_n_5e910917 c5b6f7b1ea811195.

5. Lila Abu-Lughod, "The Muslim Woman: The Power of Images and the Danger of Pity," *Eurozine*, September 1, 2006, https:// www.eurozine.com/the-muslim-woman.

6. John Eligon, "Michael Brown Spent Last Weeks Grappling with Problems and Promise," *New York Times*, August 24, 2014, https://www.nytimes.com/2014/08/25/us/michael-brown-spent -last-weeks-grappling-with-lifes-mysteries.html.

AMERICAN IDIOLECT

1. Marcie Bianco, "Queer Writing and the Strictures of Identity Politics," *Lambda Literary*, February 4, 2014, https://www.lambdaliterary .org/2014/02/queer-writing-and-the-strictures-of-identity-politics.

2. *The Punk Singer*, dir. Sini Anderson, prod. Sundance Selects, 2013.

3. *The Punk Singer*.

4. Elizabeth Chin, "Ethnically Correct Dolls: Toying with the Race Industry," *American Anthropologist* 101 (1999): 305–19.

5. Audre Lorde, "The Master's Tools Will Never Dismantle the Master's House," in *Sister Outsider: Essays and Speeches* (orig. 1984; Berkeley, CA: Crossing Press, 2007), 110–14.

POSITIVIST MENTAL ATTITUDE

1. James Hamblin, "The Paradox of Effort: A Medical Case Against Too Much Self-Control," *Atlantic*, July 16, 2015, https://www .theatlantic.com/health/archive/2015/07/the-health-cost-of-upward -mobility/398486. Italics in the original.

2. Gwendolyn Brooks, "We Real Cool," Poetry Foundation, https://www.poetryfoundation.org/poetrymagazine/poems/28112 /we-real-cool, accessed September 13, 2020.

WHATEVER PEOPLE SAY I AM, THAT'S WHAT OMNAUT

1. "2pac-Interview Outside Court House," YouTube video, 2:41, posted by 2pacshakur, April 18, 2012, https://youtu.be/j9KNnml6USQ.

2. David Mikkelson, "Trayvon Martin Photos: Photographs Purportedly Showing Shooting Victim Trayvon Martin Are Actually Pictures of Other People," *Snopes*, March 2012, https://www.snopes .com/fact-check/false-trayvon-martin-photographs.

3. Amandla Stenberg, "Don't Cash Crop on My Cornrows," YouTube video, 4:29, posted by *Hype Hair Magazine*, April 15, 2015, https://www.youtube.com/watch?v=O1KJRRSB_XA.

4. Ben Lerner, "Contest of Words," *Harper's Magazine*, October 2012, https://harpers.org/archive/2012/10/contest-of-words.

5. Robert Boynton, "Obama and the Blues: Princeton Scholar Cornel West on the Myth of 'Post-Racial Politics—and Obama's Place in History," *Rolling Stone*, March 20, 2008, https://www.rolling stone.com/culture/culture-news/obama-and-the-blues-240917.